Islam and the Ancient Mysteries

Volume One

The Mystery Schools

MAURICE HINES

MAURCHIVES & KNOWLEDGE QUEST INK

New Jersey, USA

Maurchives.com

ISBN: 979-8-9867138-1-6

Maurchives

بسم الله الرحمن الرحيم

Acknowledgements

Much appreciation to my friends, teachers, and mentors who gave me the tools and courage to compose this book: Solomon Burnette (Solayman Idris), Hatem al-Ansari, Rodrigo Adem, Rasul Miller, Ahmad Ferguson, Bayan Abdul Bari, and Imam Talib Abdul Rashid.

To my ancestors and predecessors, who taught me knowledge of self and history. To the elders in my family and community, who nurtured me and taught me life. To my peers, progeny, and future beneficiaries of this knowledge; I write this book with you in my mind and my heart.

Table Of Contents

Table Of Contents IV

An Initiation 8

SABIANS 13
ḤANĪFS 17
OVERVIEW 23

Chapter One: The Mystery Schools 26

DEFINING THE MYSTERIES 27
RELIGION OR SCHOOLS? 29
TRAITS OF THE MYSTERIES 32

Chapter Two: The Mysteries In History 37

THE DECLINE OF THE MYSTERIES 39
CHRISTIANITY AND THE MYSTERIES 43
ISLAM AND THE MYSTERIES 48

Chapter Three: The Mystery Milieu 57

ḤARRĀNIANS 59
MANDAEANS 64
NĀṢORAEANS 67
ARAB NAṢĀRĀ AND YAHŪD 72
ANCIENT EGYPTIANS 80
MAJŪS 88

Islam and the Ancient Mysteries

AN INITIATION

> "
>
> *During the Persian, Greek and Roman invasions, large numbers of Egyptians fled not only to the desert and mountain regions, but also to adjacent lands in Africa, Arabia and Asia Minor, where they lived, and secretly developed the teachings which belonged to their mystery system. In the 8th century A.D. the Moors, i.e., natives of Mauritania in North Africa, invaded Spain and took with them, the Egyptian culture which they had preserved. Knowledge in the ancient days was centralized i.e., it belonged to a common parent and system, i.e., the Wisdom Teaching or Mysteries of Egypt, which the Greeks used to call Sophia.*
>
> *George G.M. James, Stolen Legacy, 32*

If I said that the Mystery Schools was mentioned in the Qur'an, you might consider this a stretch. But if I were to ask the average reader of the Qur'an who were the *Ṣābi'ūn* mentioned in the verses *al-Baqarah*: 62, *al-Mā'idah*: 69, and *al-Ḥajj*: 17, I probably would not receive a definitive answer. Yet upon deeper research into the classical literary heritage of the Arab and Muslim world, we would find parallels between the Sabians and the Greco-Roman, Egyptian, and Persian mystery schools. Those Arabic writers described the Sabians as a religious persuasion that did not conform to many of the universal doctrines we identify with the Abrahamic traditions such as the devotion to a singular benevolent transcendent deity who is also concerned with creation, the non-eternity of the universe, salvation by God's grace, the authority of human prophets, and a moral obligation to submit to the divine law.

For over twenty years, I have pondered the connection between Islam and the Ancient Mystery Schools. While reading *Stolen Legacy: Greek Philosophy is Stolen Egyptian Philosophy* by George G. M. James, originally published in 1954, the quote at the top of this chapter caught my eye concerning Islam and the Mystery Schools. The author does not use the word Islam at all throughout the book and makes no use of Arabic texts. However, he alludes to Muslim civilization in certain parts of his book. *Stolen Legacy* represents one of the pivotal works of the African-centered study of history, whose thesis is that Egypt was the source of Greek knowledge, and as an African civilization, it made major contributions to the world. This was not a popularly accepted opinion in his time, but his work was central to the Black consciousness movement and heated academic and intercultural debates that ensue until this day. However, I milk this book from a different udder. One that makes the link between Islam and the Ancient Mystery Schools.

In a section titled, "How the African Continent gave its culture to the Western World," James asserts that the Egyptian followers of the Mysteries, were displaced due to conflicts and repression in the greater Near East. This caused them to flee to remote regions within Egypt as well as into the interiors of Africa, the Arabian Peninsula, and Asia Minor (Mesopotamia). Muslims, who James calls Moors, conquered and inhabited these "adjacent lands" later from about the 8th century until current times.[1]

His reference to the Moors, an archaic term for North African Muslims and their civilization, prompted me to study Islam from a historical perspective and eventually from a spiritual perspective. James' theory is loaded with meaning and implications despite his lack of detail for over a thousand years of history. I set out to discover what happened during this gap in history, which can be filled by a balanced reading of the development of Christianity and how these issues fed into the early history of Islam from its rise in late Antiquity to its spread during the Middle Ages in the area once known as the Roman and Persian empires and beyond. This should be put in perspective of what we know of the so-called "Mystery Schools," whose origins lie in the ancient world.

The implications of this study are that: 1) we will have a deeper and more accurate understanding of the debates and events that divided various religious movements, 2) we will witness a more contextualized religious history of the Near East from early Christianity to Medieval Islam, and 3) we will unravel much of the Islamic nomenclature used to identify various versions of the Mystery School/Sabian phenomenon. Beyond this current volume, I also wish to demonstrate how the beliefs of the Mystery Schools manifest in current times and how we can better understand where these thought currents originate.

---

[1] George G.M. James, *Stolen Legacy: Greek Philosophy Is Stolen Egyptian Philosophy* (New York: Philosophical Library, 1954), 32.

In the beginning of my exploration, I consulted Masonic and Theosophical literature on the Mystery Schools, since relatively few academics publish on the topic. James relies on this body of esoteric literature for part of his argument. I read a wide selection of this literature, but I admittedly did not fully understand Islam's relationship to the Mystery Schools until I dove into Arabic texts that discussed the identity of the *Ṣābi'ūn* or Sabians. Alas! I had found the smoking gun. The texts of pre-modern scholars who wrote in Arabic described the *Ṣābi'ūn* in the same manner esoteric sources discuss the Mysteries.

I reviewed the exegetical works of al-Ṭabarī, al-Qurṭubī, Ibn Kathīr, and Ibn Taymīyah, who all gave legal rulings on sects they identified as Sabians, primarily located in Asia Minor and Southern Iraq. They were often described as monotheistic angel worshipers and occasionally star worshipers; an odd claim from a Muslim perspective, which deems the worship of anything other than God as *shirk* (polytheism). Muslim historians like Ibn al-Nadīm and Ṣāʿid al-Andalusī, as well as polymaths like al-Shahrastānī and al-Bīrūnī fleshed out the concept of Sabianism using the sources they had access to at their times. Ibn al-Nadīm related stories of Sabian cults in Ḥarran, while al-Andalusī characterized them as the ancient religion of the world. Al-Shahrastānī investigated their books and provided a rationale of Sabian beliefs that begins with God's transcendence, angel worship, astral worship, idol worship, cyclical time, and reincarnation. Al-Bīrūnī posited his view of the Sabians as syncretic religious movements; primarily those emanating from the Jews of Babylon, who retained influences of the Chaldean religion.

In the spring of 2022, I devoted the first four months of the year to completing my master's thesis in Islamic Studies on the topic of the

Sabians. The cryptic title, *Interpretatio Islamica and the Unraveling of the Ancient Sabian Mysteries*, understandably raised some eyebrows. As I completed my academic thesis, I also publicly summarized some of my findings in the "Islam and the Ancient Mysteries" series on my personal blog, maurchives.com. Most readers scholars or otherwise have never heard of the Mystery Schools, let alone the Sabians. So, establishing the connection requires a good amount of background and context. Additionally, I built upon a concept that helped me to explain what happens when these religious communities met, which is referred to as *interpretatio*, a cultural phenomenon observed in ancient civilizations by which one culture interprets and translates the beliefs and practices of another into their own language and religion. I sought to fill the gap in scholarship that explored *interpretatio Graeca*, *Romana*, *Iranica*, and *Christiana*, but not *interpretatio Islamica* as of yet.

There is no doubt that any discussion about these topics requires a lengthy introduction. So, my goal in this volume is to explain my understanding of the Mystery Schools from an historical perspective and establish their connection to the Sabians, which I explored in some depth in the thesis. Prior to approving my thesis, my committee suggested that I remove about fifty pages from the original 150 pages for methodological reasons. The bulk of the thesis consisted of a literary analysis of Arabic texts, while the removed fifty pages consisted of an interdisciplinary historical analysis, which served as the critical cornerstone of the thesis. Since those pages were removed, I decided to use them as the basis of this book.

In this volume, I expand on the history I initially included in the thesis, which is guided by James' statement mentioned above. While some may criticize his work because it relies on esoterica, has a racialized argument, and is primarily cited by Afrocentrists, I find many of his points to be supported by adequate evidence and logic, making his above-mentioned claim worthy of investigation. I can acknowledge his shortcomings without throwing the baby out with the bathwater. Furthermore, I am not prejudiced against any genre of scholarship if the information has merit. In this study, one can say that I am applying the statement attributed to the Prophet Muhammad, "Knowledge is the lost property of the believer. Wherever he finds it, he is the most deserving of it."

Sabians

While the Sabians[2] are mentioned only three times in the Qur'an, inserted between other groups with whom we are more familiar (i.e., Jews, Christians, and Magians), they are very easy to overlook. Additionally, both past and present scholars have presented various perspectives on their identity and what they believed, perhaps obfuscating their identity even more. Contemporary Western scholars believe that the classical Muslim scholars were perplexed by this group and differed about who they were, what they believed, and their status in relation to the Muslim community. Many contemporary scholars have tried to solve this puzzle,

[2] Note that I am not referring to the Yemeni kingdom of *Saba'* (سبأ), a cognate to Sheba, for which the 34th chapter of the Qur'an is named. The Arabic spelling for the group to which I refer throughout this book begins with the letter *ṣād* (ص) and is written as Sabian in Western scholarship, whereas the Yemeni kingdom begins with the letter *sīn* (س) and is spelled Sabaean in Western scholarship.

but few have arrived at a viable conclusion. So, it remains a mystery... perhaps, a Mystery School.

In the following pages, we will dive into the secondary scholarship on the beliefs, practices, and history of Near Eastern Mystery Schools and compare them to scholarship on Sabianism. We will also place esoteric scholarship in the conversation with academic and classical scholarship on ancient religion. We will end by concluding that the Mysteries – as referred to by the Greeks, and later the Freemasons and other New Age groups – are what classical Islamic sources refer to as *Ṣābi'ah* (Sabianism),[3] a complex and multifarious religious tradition that merged different fields of knowledge into its spiritual worldview. Like the Ancient Mysteries described in modern esoteric sources, classical Muslim scholars deemed Sabianism to be the primordial religion of mankind dating back to Adam. It is most often associated with the teachings of Hermes, whose name is Tehuti or Thoth in ancient Egypt, Enoch in the Bible, and Idrīs in the Qur'an.

Over time Sabianism suffered from distortions, experienced internal reform, and became confined to an initiated minority. As Sabianism split into different factions and absorbed various languages and cultures, local prophets and sages began to reform it. This led to their obfuscation even more. One scholar examined the evidence for the various accounts of

---

[3] Throughout this book, I will use the Mystery Schools and Mysteries synonymously with Sabianism. These are general terms for this singular phenomenon, which I will specify in more detail in "Chapter Three: The Mystery Milieu."

early Muslim encounters with Sabians according to the listing of Jacques Waardenburg. The list is as follows:

- Mazdaeans of Mesopotamia, Iran and Transoxania
- Christians of various denominations
    - Nestorians of Mesopotamia and Iran
    - Monophysites of greater Syria, Egypt, and Armenia
    - Orthodox Melkites of greater Syria
    - Orthodox Latins of North Africa
    - Arians of Spain
- Jews of Mesopotamia and Iran, greater Syria, and Egypt
- Samaritans of Palestine
- Mandaeans of south Mesopotamia
- Ḥarrānians of north Mesopotamia
- Manichaeans of Mesopotamia and Egypt
- Buddhists and Hindus of the Sind
- Indigenous religions of East Africa[4]

Were the early Muslims so oblivious that they traveled the world calling every unfamiliar religious denomination Sabians or did their understanding of the term differ from ours? My view is that we can deduce the specific beliefs and identities of the Sabians if we accept that they were the remnants of the Mystery Schools. We can arrive at this fact by investigating the Near Eastern history of religion of Antiquity; its

---

[4] Christopher Buck, "The Identity of the Sabi'un: An Historical Quest," *The Muslim World* 74, no. 3–4 (1984): 172–73.

Gnostic movements, theological positions, and religious-motivated violence. This will lead us closer to revealing the mystery of the Sabians.

Therefore, my argument is that the word *ṣābi'* (Sabian) was the Arabic term for a follower of any expression of the Near Eastern ancient religion. More specifically, it could mean an initiate in one of the various "mystery cults" of the ancient world. In this manner, *ṣābi'* is synonymous with the Greek term, *mystes,* an initiate in an ancient Greek "cult" known as the *mystai* (the Mysteries). Walter Burkert calls the Mysteries a "votive religion," which is defined as a personal and voluntary religion in which one vows to follow as a means of "salvation through closeness to the divine."[5] These cults required the initiate to study various branches of knowledge (usually in secret) and perform rituals as a metaphysical manifestation of their knowledge. We will take a closer look at how those groups identified as Sabians in classical Arabic literature (i.e., the Mandaeans, the Ḥarrānians, the ancient Egyptians, and pre-Islamic Arabs), sharing many of the characteristics of those identified as belonging to the Mystery Schools in modern sources.

Furthermore, with the advent of Islam in the Arabian Peninsula, the visages of the Mystery Schools took the form of syncretic religious sects. These sects bore resemblances to Christianity and Judaism, while also being deeply influenced by Gnosticism, Neo-Platonism, Magianism, and other occult philosophies. Classical Muslim scholars grew to know these

---

[5] Walter Burkert, *Ancient Mystery Cults* (Cambridge: Harvard University Press, 1987), 12.

groups as Sabians. With regards to the term "syncretism," Jan Bremmer makes a worthy observation:

> *Most scholars today are rather hesitant about using the term, as they have become increasingly aware that all religions constantly borrow elements from other religions or ideologies: there are no 'pure' religions.*[6]

However, I contend that for Christians and Muslims, the most important thing was not just having a pure or original religion. It was about following the genuine teachings of a true prophet of God, which the Qur'an describes as the way of the Ḥanīf. The Ḥanīfs believed that by following their prophets, they could learn the true and unaltered doctrine that came directly from God. Let us demonstrate just how crucial these concepts are to our understanding of scripture.

Ḥanīfs

Ḥanīf (plural *ḥunafā'*) is another enigmatic term in the Qur'an, commonly associated with the religion of Abraham. Its root in Arabic means to incline or decline and a related word, *ḥanaf*, refers to the condition of club foot in which the foot of an infant appears abnormally twisted. The word *ḥanputā* is its cognate in Syriac for which the Near Eastern scholar, François de Blois, discusses at length across various Semitic languages.

---

[6] Jan N. Bremmer, *Initiation into the Mysteries of the Ancient World*, Münchner Vorlesungen Zu Antiken Welten 1 (Boston: De Gruyter, 2014), 117.

He states that in Syriac it carries the meaning of "pagan." In Jewish Aramaic it means "to deceive" or "to flatter." Mandaic variations of the word allude to "the worship of false gods" and "hypocrite." It also carries these meanings in Hebrew as well as "to pollute" and "to be polluted."[7]

Beyond the linguistic *deceptae*, why would Abraham and his *ḥanafīyah* be associated with polytheism? After all, would the Jewish, Christian, and polytheist Qur'anic interlocutors not already acknowledge him as a patriarch of monotheism?.[8] In light of de Blois's presentation of Semitic cognates to *ḥanīf*, it becomes clear that the majority of the Qur'an's interlocutors probably associated *ḥanafīyah* with polytheism. And so, it is important to remember that in the context of the region, 7th century Arabia, not unlike the greater Near East, was heavily influenced by Sabian thought. As such, we cannot assume that our contemporary understandings about Biblical and Qur'anic figures were always understood in the manner we understand them today. In fact, people like Noah, Abraham, Moses, and Jesus were very controversial, and their lives and mission necessitated divine vindication to absolve them of the lies and distortions their narratives had undergone. In *al-Aḥzāb*: 7, God says

---

[7] François de Blois, "Naṣrānī (Ναζωραῖος) and Ḥanīf (Ἐθνικός): Studies on the Religious Vocabulary of Christianity and of Islam," *Bulletin of the School of Oriental and African Studies, University of London* 65, no. 1 (2002): 19.

[8] *See* Qur'an: *al-Baqarah*: 135, *Āli ʿImrān*: 67 and 95, *al-Anʿām*: 79 and 161, *Yūnus*: 105, *al-Naḥl*: 120 and 123, *al-Ḥajj*: 31, and *al-Bayyinah*: 5. All ten of these verses provide additional clarification to the word *ḥanīf*, negating its association with polytheism.

that He has taken a covenant from the four prophets mentioned above to question the truthful ones about their truthfulness and to prepare a painful punishment for the disbelievers. These are exactly the prophets that certain Sabian groups rejected, but I will only focus on Abraham here.

If we read the Qur'an more closely, we will find twelve instances of the word *ḥanīf* or *ḥunafā'*, most of them in reference to the Prophet Abraham, contrasting him to the *mushrikūn* (polytheists). In *al-Naḥl*: 120, for instance, the Qur'an states: *Indeed, Abraham was an ummah,*[9] *obedient to God as a Ḥanīf, and he was not of the polytheists*. It appears to be common knowledge for anyone receiving the words of this verse that Abraham was not a polytheist. So, why is the elaboration needed?

Again, if we consider the whole picture of what was happening in the Near East during the 7th century, we will find a myriad of alternate narratives about the prophets that was propagated by various Sabian groups. These narratives would make it difficult to clearly uncover the original stories of these prophets. Some of them taught that Abraham, the strongest antagonist to the Chaldean Sabians of Babylon, aspired to become a high priest in their religion. However, he came under the possession of an evil spirit named Yūrbā who overpowered him to circumcise himself. As mentioned in *al-Fihrist*, the Sabians believed that missing any part of the body or illness rendered a person impure, and thus

---

[9] Most Qur'anic exegetes are of the opinion that *ummah* means "leader" in this verse rather than "religious community." Referring to a single person as an *ummah* carries a stronger meaning than using any of the conventional words for leader. It implies that Abraham as an individual embodied all the other qualities associated with the word: nation, epoch, religion, and leader.

Abraham was no longer qualified for the position of high priest. Instead, they claimed that he became an outcast followed by lepers, amputees, and other reprobates. Yūrbā gave him magical powers to make him invincible to fire. He then, in the name of Yūrbā, attacked the peaceful Sabians of Babylon, forcibly circumcising the men and compelling them to join his religion.[10]

The Qur'an is obviously seeking to clarify a narrative that was once misunderstood and continues to be misunderstood. The story of Abraham has even confused some Muslim exegetes, who find it difficult to remove him from allegations of a polytheistic phase based on the verses in *al-An'ām*: 75-85, in which he supposedly praises the stars, moon, and sun as deities. I believe there is more than meets the eye regarding these verses, but it requires a familiarity with Sabianism in the Near East to understand what these verses are actually trying to convey.

The apparent meaning of these verses is that Abraham admonishes his people for idolatry, then embarks on a spiritual quest in which he declares the celestial bodies as his lord. It is only once he notices each of them dissipate that he realizes God transcends His creation. Many interpretations of this conclude that this was a phase of spiritual exploration Abraham undertook in his youth before prophethood. But it raises a series of questions that need to be addressed. Would this phase of spiritual exploration and astral worship not nullify Abraham's infallibility? From an Islamic perspective, is a prophet not chosen from

---

[10] ʿAbdullah ʿAlī Samak, *Al-Ṣābi'ūn*, 1st ed. (Cairo: Maktabat al-Ādāb, 1995), 42–43.

birth and shielded from all forms of idolatry until he realizes his prophetic mission? If so, why must Abraham burden himself with a spiritual quest? Why does he admonish his people for worshiping idols and celestial bodies – as was the custom among the Chaldeans – only to indulge in his own form of idolatry? Was he not yet secure in his faith? Furthermore, he would have witnessed the sun, moon, and stars fade daily; so why was he surprised by their fading only at that point in time? We can easily resolve these questions when we take a look at the situation through a different lens, by understanding the Sabian influence that led to the revelation of such verses.

It is possible that the Sabians recognized Abraham as one of their scholars or priests. But they would not recognize him as a messenger or prophet of God, whose teachings the people should follow. As a result, God emphasizes that Abraham as an individual functions as a leader, religion, community, and nation as evidenced in *al-Baqarah*: 124 and *al-Naḥl*: 120.[11] The Sabians only acknowledge angels as messengers, not men. So, they naturally rejected his claim to prophethood or any type of religious authority beyond the clerical status quo.

As for Abraham's spiritual quest, God in *al-An'ām*: 85, showed Abraham the dominion (*malakūt*) of the heavens and the earth. On this verse al-Qurṭubī states: "It is said that God unveiled for [the Prophet Abraham] the heavens and the earth to the level of the Throne [of God] and the lower worlds (or under worlds)." Similarly, he cites a chain of Islamic authorities who said, "The seven heavens were opened to him. He gazed at them until it reached the Throne. Then the lands were opened up and he gazed at them. He also saw his place in *jannah* [i.e., heaven]." Al-Qurṭubī then states that al-Ḍaḥḥāk believed the dominion of the heavens to be what Abraham saw of the stars and the dominion of the earth to be the seas, mountains, vegetation, and the like.[12]

Verse 85 asserts that God allowed a human prophet to traverse the heavens and gaze upon His Throne. For the Sabians, this station is reserved only for the angels who occupy the forms of the stars and planets. Given mankind's continued fascination with outer space, we can easily relate to how awe-struck Abraham must have been to encounter the terrestrial and celestial *malakūt* first-hand. Upon witnessing the secrets of the sun, moon, and stars out of astonishment he exclaimed, "This is my Lord!" However, he did not mean to deify these bodies with his expression, as many Qur'anic exegetes and laypeople believe. His expression contains an ellipsis (*iḍmār*), a literary device in which a word is purposefully omitted for rhetorical effect. So, Abraham's statement may be equivalent to "this is *the dominion* of my lord!" or "this is *the evidence* of my lord!"[13] After witnessing these celestial bodies in all their grandeur dissipate, Abraham then understands the magnanimity of the

---

[12] Qurṭubī, *Al-Jāmi'*, vol. 7, 23-4.

[13] Out of all the well-known exegetes of the Qur'an, only al-Qurṭubī recorded this position, although it might not have been his choice opinion. It is the last thing he mentions after a lengthy discussion about Abraham entertaining polytheistic notions. *Al-Jāmi'*, vol. 7, 27.

God, who created these magnificent structures then caused them to vanish. At that moment, he recognized that God never dissipates and thus became a *Ḥanīf* by turning his face to the One who originated all things.

Unlike Sabian worship of celestial bodies, the result of Abraham's exposure to these wonders was not that he acknowledged their divinity, but it increased his certainty that they were not deities. In Abraham's dispute with his people in *al-Anʿām:* 81, we can draw a clear line between an upright Ḥanīf and idolatrous Sabian: a Ḥanīf opposes associating anything with God, regardless of its impressiveness, while a Sabian is inclined to deify the things with which he is impressed. Rhetorically, God asks which of these two groups is more secure in their faith? Is it the one who worships the creation or the Creator?

Overview

Now that we gained some insights into the Sabian – Ḥanīf dichotomy in Islamic scripture, we can start to make the connection to the Mystery Schools that rivaled the previous Ḥanīf system, Christianity. However, before embarking on our discussion on the Mystery Schools in the Christian era, let us quickly review how classical Muslim exegetes, jurists, historians, and theologians have characterized the Sabians and their religion[14]:

---

[14] I covered Islamic views of the Sabians more extensively in my master's thesis. *See* "*Interpretatio Islamica* and the Unraveling of the Ancient Sabian Mysteries" (American University in Cairo, 2023), https://fount.aucegypt.edu/etds/2052.

1. They follow a religion that resembles the other religions mentioned in the Qur'an (Judaism, Christianity, and Zoroastrianism) in that they are monotheistic, adhere to a scripture, and practice ritual fasting and praying.

2. They are associated with the worship of the angels and celestial bodies.

3. They are associated with philosophy and advanced knowledge of astrology.

4. Although their religion used to be widespread on earth especially in Babylon, India, Egypt, as well as pre-Islamic Arabia, the last recognizable traces of Sabians in lands conquered by Muslims can be found in Ḥarrān (Asia Minor) and the marshes of southern Iraq and Iran.

5. The Sabians and Ḥanīfs, even though they share a common origin, represented two distinct ways of looking at theology, cosmology, prophetology, angelology, and astrology.

6. Muhammad al-Shahrastānī devised a way to classify Sabianism, placing them on a continuum between the worship of angels, celestial bodies, and idols to belief in reincarnation and pantheism.

With these points in mind, I will also present a framework that we can use to view religious conflicts and debates throughout the ages. This is the dichotomy we have witnessed in different times, places, and religions: Sabian vs. Ḥanīf, Gnostic vs. Orthodoxy, Rationalists vs. Traditionalists, etc. It has been difficult for modern minds to understand the details of religious conflict without appreciating the metaphysical and material significance these conflicts have had on the world. I seek to offer some new insights into the religious world of the past and show how they affect us to this day.

In Chapter One, I will provide a brief overview of the Mystery Schools, providing classical definitions for the Mysteries and other terms associated with them. I will expand on its nature as a widespread religious persuasion in the Near East, while also speaking to specific expressions of the Mysteries covered by previous academic authors. I will also cover the most outstanding traits of the Mysteries in terms of practice and beliefs. Chapter Two recounts the history of the Mystery Schools in Rome, starting with its decline in relation to the rise of Christianity. I will detail how this shift in power and popularity occurred from a novel perspective, as well as how the turmoil settled to one degree and persisted as the Sabian phenomenon under Islamic hegemony. Understanding this history will help us flesh out the groups that Medieval Arabic writers identified as Sabians. This is the purpose of Chapter Three in which I will attempt to connect the Ḥarrānians, the Mandaeans and their priestly class the Nāṣoraeans, Ancient Egyptians, the Majūs, as well as the Arab Naṣārā and Yahūd to each other and the Mystery Schools. Chapter Four will conclude this volume by expanding on the underlying implications and future directions of my study.

CHAPTER ONE

THE MYSTERY SCHOOLS

"

If research and reflection be pushed far enough it becomes clear that the universality and uniformity referred to are due to the fact that at one time, long back in the world's past, there existed or was implanted in the minds of the whole human family... a Proto-Evangelium or Root-Doctrine in regard to the nature and destiny of the soul of man and its relation to the Deity.
W.L. Wilmshurst, The Meaning of Masonry, 203.

Is it possible to take the mystery out of the Mystery Schools? What is their connection to the Sabians mentioned thrice in the Qur'an? And what was their role in the metaphysical debates that shaped the three Abrahamic religions? Who were the so-called Moors, who preserved and transferred the knowledge of the Mysteries to the Western European civilization as articulated by George G.M. James? I hope to provide the answers to these questions and more in the following chapters. This chapter will provide a background to the Near Eastern Mystery Schools according to academic and authoritative Freemasonic sources.

Defining the Mysteries

Prior to exploring the history, let us first understand what the Mystery Schools are. The word *mystery* is a cognate to *mysterion* in Greek, which is related to the verb *myein*, ("to close one's lips or eyes"). The Freemasonic author, Albert Mackey, relates the English term to its archaic meaning. According to him, masonic guilds and companies were called *mysteries* in the Middle Ages, because they were secret societies who sought to protect their trade secrets from those who were not members. Similarly, the terms *mystery* and *craft* were used interchangeably.[15]

As for the ancient mysteries, Marvin Meyer states that they were systems of personal salvation apart from popular religion. Their closed nature was due to the oath of secrecy a *mystes* (initiate) swore to conceal the secrets of the organizations and not divulge them to outsiders. The priest of a Greek mystery cult was called a *hierophant*, meaning "one who shows sacred objects," while a high-level initiate was called an *epoptes*, "a beholder." This was because the ceremonies were divine reenactments and displays of sacred symbols, whose meanings were only known to

---

[15] Albert G. Mackey, *An Encyclopedia of Freemasonry and Its Kindred Sciences: Comprising the Whole Range of Arts, Sciences and Literature as Connected with the Institution*, vol. 1. (New York: Masonic History Company, 1914), 500.

initiates.[16] Every initiate also had a *mystagōgos* to guide him or her in the process.[17]

This initiation was known as a "mystical death" by which the *mystes* was purified. Albert Pike, states "the perfect Epopt was then said to be regenerated, new-born, restored to a renovated existence of life, light, and purity; and placed under the Divine Protection."[18] Sarah Iles Johnston, a scholar of Greek religion, summarizes the Mystery Schools to five points: 1) they kept an oath of secrecy, 2) they had a system of salvation, 3) they established for the initiate a special relationship with the divine, 4) they were supplemental to public religion (hence the term cult by which they are sometimes referred), and 5) each one developed its own mythology.[19] Jan Bremmer gives a similar summary, only adding the points that they were always voluntary, they required purification, involved night

---

[16] Meyer, *Ancient Mysteries*, 4-5. A member of the Lesser Mysteries was called a *mystes*, while those in the Greater Mysteries were called *epoptes*. *See* Pike, *Morals and Dogma*, 500.

[17] Sarah Iles Johnston, ed., *Ancient Religions* (Cambridge, Mass: Belknap Press of Harvard University Press, 2007), 100.

[18] Pike, *Morals and Dogma*, 249.

[19] Sarah Iles Johnston, ed., *Ancient Religions* (Cambridge, Mass: Belknap Press of Harvard University Press, 2007), 98-9.

performances, there was a fee to participate, the rituals usually took place outside the city, and they were open to women, slaves, and children.[20]

Religion or Schools?

As for their attribute as schools, I believe this term to be more sophisticated than cult and more descriptive of their true nature: different schools of thought of one religion. Bremmer elucidates the different purposes of a selection of Greek Mystery Schools. For instance, she concludes that the Eleusinian Mysteries consisted of primarily fertility rituals designed to help agriculturalists yield bountiful crops,[21] while the Samothracian were designed to protect maritime travelers from the dangers at sea,[22] and the Korybantes Mysteries allowed women initiates an escapism, which freed them from phobias and anxiety.[23] One can see in this that the Mysteries attracted people of similar professional and socio-economic backgrounds for common purposes. The "schools" are where initiates learned and experienced the esoteric aspects of their otherwise material knowledge, which involved the influence of celestial bodies over earthly phenomena. In other words, it was in the Lesser

---

[20] Jan N. Bremmer, *Initiation into the Mysteries of the Ancient World*, Münchner Vorlesungen Zu Antiken Welten 1 (Boston: De Gruyter, 2014), xii.

[21] Bremmer, *Initiation*, 15.

[22] Bremmer, *Initiation*, 28-9.

[23] Bremmer, *Initiation*, 53.

Mysteries that initiates learned how to manipulate earthly phenomena such as rain, metals, and plant life, while the Greater Mysteries taught the science of stars and the heavens that governed the nature of things on earth, in accordance with the Hermetic concept, "As above, so below."[24]

With regards to their origins, Freemasons like Mackey state that it is impossible to trace the origins of the Mystery Schools because their history is veiled by symbols and their true doctrines were kept secret so as not to be distorted by "the superstitions, innovations, and corruptions of the world as it then existed." Yet, they maintain that they have a common origin.[25] Pike asserts that they encompassed the ideas that circulated through the ancient oriental civilizations, as well as those ideas of the philosophers, and that they came from the east and spread west.[26] Academic authors like Burkert, for instance, would also argue that they have an ancient origin. However, he does not believe they were necessarily "oriental" (i.e., eastern) in nature or that they were simply "spiritual" alternatives to popular religion. Rather, he emphasizes as Fritz Graf noted, that each cult exemplified the local linguistic and cultural forms of each environment in which it was found.[27] Nevertheless, Burkert

---

[24] Rene Guenon, *Spiritual Authority and Temporal Power*, trans. Henry D. Fohr and Samuel D. Fohr (New York: Sophia Perennis, 1929), 22.

[25] Mackey, *Encyclopedia of Freemasonry*, vol. 1, 497.

[26] Pike, *Morals and Dogma*, 248.

[27] Walter Burkert, *Ancient Mystery Cults* (Cambridge: Harvard University Press, 1987), 2-3 and Fritz Graf in Johnston, *Ancient Religions*, 7.

concludes in the following statement that they were all part of one "conglomerate:"

> *Whereas in these religions [i.e. Judaism, Christianity, and Islam] there has been much conscious emphasis on self-definition and on demarcating one religion as against the other, in the pre-Christian epoch the various forms of worship, including new and foreign gods in general and the institution of mysteries in particular, are never exclusive; they appear as varying forms, trends, or options within the one disparate yet continuous conglomerate of ancient religion.*[28]

Were we to ponder Burkert's "conglomerate" characterization, we would find that there were many iterations of the Mysteries in the ancient world based on regional and liturgical differences. There were the Eleusinian, Orphic, Bacchic, Dionysiac, and other local Mysteries of Greece, as well as the Egyptian Isis and Persian Mithraic Mysteries. They all overlapped in some basic respects, as described by Johnston and Bremmer, yet they also possessed their own distinctive traits by which they were known.

To Burkert's point about their lack of exclusivity, this is because they believed that there was only one religion, but one's cultural expression of it was tied to their citizenship.[29] Intercultural religious differences were

---

[28] Burkert, *Ancient*, 4.

[29] Clifford Ando, "Religious Affiliation and Political Belonging from Cicero to Theodosius," *Acta Classica* 64, no. 1 (2021), 13.

minimized through the process of *interpretatio*, in which one culture or religion translated beliefs and practices from another into their own language, culture, and religion. On the other hand, the perceived exclusivity of the Abrahamic traditions is not entirely true. The Abrahamic traditions agree on their root doctrines which affirm a personal deity, authority of the prophets, and salvation by grace. However, the differences between them were the result of the degree to which they embraced aspects of the Mysteries. Nevertheless, it suffices us to say that most scholars who have written on the topic are of one accord that the Mystery Schools had a common origin and similar characteristics.

Traits of the Mysteries

Some prevalent characteristics of the Mysteries worth noting are that there were two main levels, the Lesser and Greater Mysteries. The Lesser Mysteries are the basis for initiation, which prepares the aspirant morally for the deeper metaphysical training he acquires in the Greater Mysteries.[30] One also finds that initiates in the Mysteries forego certain types of foods.[31] Similarly, they had strict standards of moral and physical

---

[30] Rene Guenon, *Spiritual Authority and Temporal Power*, trans. Henry D. Fohr and Samuel D. Fohr (New York: Sophia Perennis, 1929), 22, and Rene Guenon, *Perspectives on Initiation*, ed. Samuel D. Fohr, trans. Henry D. Fohr (New York: Sophia Perennis, 1946), 18.

[31] Johnston, *Ancient Religions*, 104, and Bremmer, *Initiation*, 66, 117. The Sabians forbade themselves from eating pigs, dogs, and donkeys, in addition to

purity for their initiates. For instance, a Stoic sage had to be perfect in every way. He was serious, virtuous, and proper. To them, "health, strength, and soundness of the senses were in accordance with nature" whereas "sickness, weakness, and mutilation were contrary to nature."[32] This corresponds to the description of Ibn al-Nadīm concerning the Sabian view of prophethood:

> *They say that a man who is an announcer of God (al-nabi) is he who is free from evil in his soul and from imperfections of the body, who is perfect in everything praiseworthy, who does not fall short in answering every question correctly, who tells what is in the imaginings, whose prayer for rain is answered, who wards off pests*

---

birds with talons and vegetables like legumes, beans, garlic, lentils, green beans, cauliflower, and cabbage.

[32] Stock, *Stoicism*, 52-3. James gives ten virtuous principles required of any initiate: "(I) control his thoughts (II) control his actions (III) have devotion of purpose (IV) have faith in the ability of his master to teach him the truth (V) have faith in himself to assimilate the truth (VI) have faith in himself to wield the truth (VII) be free from resentment under the experience of persecution (VIII) be free from resentment under experience of wrong, (IX) cultivate the ability to distinguish between right and wrong and (X) cultivate the ability to distinguish between the real and the unreal (he must have a sense of values)." James, *Stolen Legacy*, 77.

> *from plants and animals, and whose doctrine improves the world, increasing its population.*[33]

Moreover, initiates in the Mysteries were expected to master various sciences, chief among them was the science of the stars. James gathers from the works of Diodorus, Herodotus and Clement of Alexandria that the Egyptian Mysteries had six orders, each specializing in a selection of the books of Hermes. Several of these focus on astronomy and astrology, but also topics such as geography, anatomy, theology, law, etc. The primary incentive for joining the mysteries was not only salvation, but as James describes it, to transcend the fetters of their bodies and ascend to the levels of the gods through rigorous studies of the arts and sciences.[34]

Some other traits of the Mysteries, as seen by their Ḥanīf adversaries, are of a philosophical nature. These traits are most succinctly found in the Gnostic and philosophical literature of Antiquity. Gnosticism is by nature a secretive tradition and one that has been compelled to go underground due to aspects of their beliefs and practices. In my readings of Sabianism and Gnosticism I have extracted the following characteristics as the main points of contentions with Ḥanīfs:[35]

---

[33] Abū al-Faraj Muḥammad ibn Isḥaq Ibn al-Nadīm, *The Fihrist of Al-Nadim: A Tenth Century Survey of Muslim Culture*, trans. Bayard Dodge, vol. 2 (New York: Columbia University Press, 1970), 749.

[34] James, *Stolen Legacy*, 7, 95-9.

[35] Robert M. Grant, *Gnosticism and Early Christianity*, Lectures on the History of Religions (New York: Columbia University Press, 1959), 15–19.

1. Eternity of the universe
2. Status of the angels
3. Salvation through knowledge

The eternity of the universe may seem insignificant, but it has been one of the most contentious issues for Jews, Christians, and Muslims against their Sabian antagonists. Without diving into the details of this controversy and the particular instances of these arguments throughout history, the Sabians argue that the universe has no creator and that time and the universe are eternal. In contrast, the Ḥanīf contends that the universe and time are not eternal but are the creation of God. The implications of the Sabian position are that God is not the creator of the universe and that it is possible for God to be part of the creation. This is problematic to Ḥanīf sensibilities because it permits the notion of pantheism and anthropomorphism.

The personification and worship of angels is another salient trait of Sabianism, as evidenced in the Gnostic writings of antiquity as well as in the earliest Islamic descriptions of Sabianism. Although most Sabians profess a belief in one supreme God, some deny that God is the creator of the universe. Instead, they believe that angels or lesser deities created the universe and tell elaborate creation myths. These myths were often used as wisdom teachings to explain nuanced aspects of theology and ethics. On the other hand, these myths have also led to the deification of angels and hence the acceptance of polytheism.

As for salvation, they believed that knowledge was the only way. This refers to empirical and occult knowledge but chiefly knowledge of the self and the realization of themselves as divine. It was common for them to believe that the origin of human beings was the higher spirit world and that they were simply incorporeal spirits caught in corporeal bodies. Salvation, thus, meant to break the cycle of the lowly physical world of sensory perception and carnal desires through self-knowledge that hastened their ascent to be truly "born again" in the spiritual world. Grant states more precisely that traditional religions were God-centered whereas Gnosticism (i.e., Sabianism) was self-centered. As such, the Gnostic and philosophical expressions of the Mysteries emphasized a rigorous ascetism to distance the initiate from the fetters of the body as well as human freedom from what they perceived to be the tyranny of men, law, and religion.[36]

The traits of the Mysteries are not lost on us now. Many New Age spiritual gurus teach these doctrines and encourage this outlook. With these noble aims, why did Christianity oppose the Mysteries? In the next chapter, we will explore the history of the conflict between Christianity and the Mystery Schools and how they were reconciled by some Christians. We will also explore how these conflicts fed into early Islamic history and the Muslim response to them.

---

[36] Robert M. Grant, *Gnosticism and Early Christianity*, Lectures on the History of Religions (New York: Columbia University Press, 1959), 7–12.

CHAPTER TWO

The Mysteries in History

"

كَانَ ٱلنَّاسُ أُمَّةً وَٰحِدَةً فَبَعَثَ ٱللَّهُ ٱلنَّبِيِّـۧنَ مُبَشِّرِينَ وَمُنذِرِينَ وَأَنزَلَ مَعَهُمُ ٱلْكِتَـٰبَ بِٱلْحَقِّ لِيَحْكُمَ بَيْنَ ٱلنَّاسِ فِيمَا ٱخْتَلَفُوا۟ فِيهِ ۚ وَمَا ٱخْتَلَفَ فِيهِ إِلَّا ٱلَّذِينَ أُوتُوهُ مِنۢ بَعْدِ مَا جَآءَتْهُمُ ٱلْبَيِّنَـٰتُ بَغْيًۢا بَيْنَهُمْ ۖ فَهَدَى ٱللَّهُ ٱلَّذِينَ ءَامَنُوا۟ لِمَا ٱخْتَلَفُوا۟ فِيهِ مِنَ ٱلْحَقِّ بِإِذْنِهِۦ ۗ وَٱللَّهُ يَهْدِى مَن يَشَآءُ إِلَىٰ صِرَٰطٍ مُّسْتَقِيمٍ

Mankind was one ummah [religious community]; then God sent the prophets as bringers of hope and as warners. He sent them down with the Scripture in truth to arbitrate between people concerning that in which they differed. And no one differed in the Scripture except those who were given it after clear proofs came to them due to jealous animosity between them. Therefore, God guided those who believed to the truth of what they differed in, by His permission. And God guides whom He wills to a straight path. (al-Baqarah: 213)

This verse and others like it from the Qur'an clearly indicate that there was only one original religion of mankind, to which all people adhered. After which, people disputed among themselves about particulars and this disputation led to factionalism and the multitude of religious expressions we have today. The saving grace was the prophets and sages that appeared at the height of various epochs to reaffirm those universal teachings. This runs counter to the evolutionary view on the origins of religion, which is accepted as a matter of fact in many academic publications as well as in popular culture.

The evolutionary view posits that humans created religion in a long process that commenced with animism, ancestral worship, the worship of nature, and heavenly bodies; then their beliefs became progressively more abstract, eventually culminating in monotheistic or atheistic religions. Yet, the vast majority of ancient religions say otherwise, claiming a pure monotheistic origin as the Qur'anic verse above and many other scriptures and folkloric creation myths indicate.

The primordial religion of mankind is a single phenomenon that goes by different names depending on the language and locale. The Greeks knew it as *Mystai* (the Mysteries), the Indians called it *Sanātana Dharma* (the Eternal Way), the ancient Iranians called it *Asha* or *Mazda*, the monotheistic Arabs called it *Ḥanīfīyah* while polytheistic Arabs knew it as *Ṣābi'ah,* and some now know it as *Sophia Perennis* (the Perennial Wisdom). Though their origins were pure and sanctified, according to the Abrahamic narrative, they eventually devolved into corruption and error.

While the origin of all religions is one, two major factions began to develop over time. One faction, at times known as Hanifs, Orthodox, or Traditionalists, held on to its original monotheistic creed and the other, known as Sabians, Gnostics, or Spiritualists, innovated ideas that deviated from the creed of monotheism and claimed that God was too transcendent to be worshiped directly and required intercessors by which their worship is transferred to God. This is demonstrated by the Qur'anic verse, *Zumar*: 3, on the tongues of the polytheists who state: "We only worship them to bring us closer to God."

Regardless of the language and local religious customs, the aberrated version of the primordial religion became known for its worshipful reverence of the stars and their personification in the form of mythical beings, which Muslims know to be either *malā'ikah* (angels) or *jinn*. The followers of these aberrated religions also built megalithic temples and other structures that aligned with celestial movements and often ornamented with pictorial writings containing doctrine, wisdom, and the stories of kings and queens. They were also known for their scientific explorations and philosophical speculations. Astronomy, the chief of their sciences, aided in their worship of the stars as well as with predictions of future events for agricultural, imperial, and individualized purposes. They often believed in the eternity of the universe and reincarnation and engaged in human sacrifice. This was the case in much of the ancient world.

Knowledge of this dichotomy has been lost to history due to many factors. The Ḥanīf faction, in the form of the Abrahamic religions Judaism, Christianity, and Islam, have managed to gain religious and political authority, which has drowned out the perspectives of the Sabian factions, made their practices of calling on spirits and conducting human sacrifices taboo if not punishable by law, and marginalized their influence in societies where the Ḥanīf doctrines dominate. In this chapter, I will attempt to explain the decline of the Mysteries under Christendom and their revival as Sabians under Islam.

The Decline of the Mysteries

The Roman Emperor, Theodosius I's official closure of the Mysteries in 391 C.E. was considered a triumph for Christianity and the death knell for the Mystery Schools in the Roman Empire whose seat lay in modern-day Turkey. Ironically, at the beginning of the 4th century, Christianity was a reviled religion in the empire, but by the end of the century was not only the official religion, but the only acceptable religion according to Roman law. How this came to be is well-documented by historians. Emperor Constantine was the first to end the persecution of Christians and establish a Christian orthodoxy through the ecumenical councils of Nicaea in 325 C.E., Constantinople in 381 C.E., and subsequent councils extending into the 6th century. Thus, Christianity was no longer a marginal religion in the empire and existed alongside the various so-called pagan cults or Mystery Schools.

Thereafter, Christianity, particularly those sects that subscribed to the Nicene Creed, would have the upper hand, forcing later emperors to either permit or restrict the activities of the Mystery Schools. Prior to Christianity, the Mysteries was the dominant religious expression throughout the empire. Even early Christian sacraments had to use the language of the Mysteries, such as *mystêrion/mysterium* for baptism.[37] However, ostentatious public festivals in honor of Jupiter and other deities would soon be repressed as more people began to embrace the moral conservatism of Christianity.

Many believe that the Mysteries were closed for malicious and sectarian reasons. James, other Afrocentric authors, and Theosophists, for instance, attempt to portray the Mysteries as completely pristine and

---

[37] Bremmer, *Initiation,* 162.

innocent institutions that fell victim to the heavy hand of overzealous Christian Roman emperors and their closure is what plunged Western Europe into the Dark Ages.[38] Yet, this should be cross-referenced with the views of Freemasons and academic scholars on the matter. Mackey notes in his *Encyclopedia of Freemasonry* that the Mysteries continued well after the rise of Christianity but suffered decline. Around the 4th century C.E., in their desire to win converts, they lowered the standards for initiation by discontinuing extensive background checks to determine if a potential aspirant was of high moral character. As such, all calibers of people were initiated indiscriminately. Very few initiates remembered the wisdom behind their rites, so they soon devolved into mere superstitions. Moreover, officiators of the Mysteries sought out fees for admitting new initiates, which led to more corruption. Mackey goes on to say that this corruption caught the attention of the Roman emperors like Constantine and Gratian, who forbade their night celebrations. According to this perspective, the Mysteries had already suffered internal corruption, and when this became a societal issue, the emperors regulated them and eventually outlawed them.[39]

---

[38] James, *Stolen Legacy,* 30, and Alfred J. Butler, *The Arab Conquest of Egypt and the Last Thirty Years of the Roman Dominion* (Oxford: Clarendon Press, 1902), 413. Renè Guenon believes the "Dark Age" of Europe to be a myth. Rather, he believes that Christianity actually revived the intellectuality of the ancient Greeks, *cf* Rene Guenon, *The Crisis of the Modern World*, trans. Marco Pallis, Arthur Osborne, and Richard C. Nicholson (New York: Sophia Perennis, 1946), 12-6.

[39] Mackey, *Encyclopedia of Freemasonry*, 500.

M.L.W. Laistner explains that throughout the 4th and 5th centuries Roman emperors issued multiple edicts banning certain popular amusements on Sunday, "the Lord's Day." The reason for this "severely puritanical tone" of church leaders on this matter was due to the brutality and obscenity that were perpetrated at these games and theaters. He goes on to quote Theodore of Mopsuetia's address to baptismal candidates in which he chastises Christians who attended the pagan ceremonies, believed in astrology, practiced magic, or frequented the theater, circus, racecourse, athletic games, and dances. Concerning the context out of which Christianity arose, Laistner states that philosophy and Mystery Cults began to resemble religious movements and speak in religious terms. At the same time, belief in astrology and magic continued to dominate the masses and became signs of people's allegiance to Sabianism, which they called paganism.[40]

We should also understand, as noted previously, that religion in Rome was a matter of citizenship. Therefore, Constantine's acceptance of Christianity put latter emperors in the tenuous position of naturalizing a foreign, previously subversive religion into the domain of legitimate Roman citizenship. On top of that, the Roman emperor also held the title of *Pontifex Maximus*, meaning that he was both the religious and secular authority. As such, he was the leader of two conflicting religions. Julian (331-363 C.E., nicknamed "the Apostate" after renouncing Christianity) would allow pagans to worship openly, welcome all Christian

[40] M.L.W. Laistner, *Christianity and Pagan Culture in the Later Roman Empire* (Ithaca, NY: Cornell University Press, 1951), 4–8.

denominations, and allow exiled bishops to return to their homes. Whereas Theodosius I (347-395 C.E.), by the end of the century, would mandate the Nicene Creed as Christian orthodoxy and ban all the practices and festivals of the Mystery Schools.[41]

Christianity and the Mysteries

In the early 20th century, some European scholars questioned the degree to which Christianity incorporated elements from the Mysteries. Although Bremmer is largely dismissive of this hypothesis, she nevertheless devotes an entire chapter to this issue. She begins the chapter by mentioning the lectures of Rudolf Steiner, a German Theosophist and founder of the Waldorf schools, who sought to draw connections between Christianity and the ancient Mysteries. Steiner posited that the mysteries go back to at least the 8th century B.C.E and took from the Mysteries of Egypt, Persia, and India. Bremmer provides further context by examining other European authors from the early 20th century who sought to draw such connections, stating that the debate was on a continuum of those who believed Christianity was wholly derived from the ancient Mysteries to those, like Eduard Meyer, who believed that Judaism was the only religion to have an influence on formative Christianity. Bremmer

---

[41] R. M. Errington, *Roman Imperial Policy from Julian to Theodosius*, Studies in the History of Greece and Rome (Chapel Hill: University of North Carolina Press, 2006), 249-52.

contends that this debate died out in the 1920's, when it was overshadowed by other theological interests.[42]

Bremmer considers the debate to be summarized by Arthur Darby Nock (1902–1963), an English expert on Greco-Roman Religion as well as Judaism and early Christianity. In his 1952 publication, *Hellenistic Mysteries and Christian Sacraments,* he explores the "mystery metaphor" and its use during the early rise of Christianity. Nock states that the Jewish philosopher, Philo, used Mystery terminology, the Wisdom of Solomon has two verses that mention the mysteries, Jesus mentions "*mystêrion*" (secret) in Mark 4:11, Paul employs Mystery terminology in the Letter to the Corinthians (2:1 and 4:1) and Letter to the Romans (11:25). However, Nock, like Bremmer, remained skeptical of any strong correlation between Christianity and the Ancient Mysteries, citing overriding doctrinal differences, negative impressions of the Mysteries by early Christians, and Christian influence on the Mysteries.[43]

While I agree that Christianity, at its core, is a Ḥanīf system, and is thus foundationally divorced from the epistemology of the Mysteries due to its emphasis on prophecy and establishing a direct relationship between humans and the Creator, my assessment of this attempt of early Christians to appropriate the language of the Mysteries is that they were entering an arena of metaphysical debates that was dominated by Mystery Schools.

---

[42] Bremmer, *Initiation,* 142-4.

[43] Bremmer, *Initiation,* 147-61.

To enter this debate, they had to engage the ideas of the Mysteries in a common language, which inevitably meant adapting some of their ideas and making a place for them in a Christian worldview.

As one might notice in modern times, Christianity has taken much from the so-called pagan Mysteries. The title of *Pontifex Maximus*, once reserved for the Holy Roman Emperor, is now reserved for the Pope of Rome.[44] Justinian closed the Neoplatonic academies in order to consolidate Roman religious thought, since their ideas resembled that of Christianity.[45] Even quintessential Christian concepts and terms such as the Trinity and Logos had been debated by philosophers prior to the Christian era.[46] Pike asserts that Christ's birth was announced by a "Star from the East" and his nativity was celebrated on the shortest day of the Julian calendar, which coincides with the festivals of Mithras in Persia and Osiris in Egypt. He also points out that formative Christian authors like Justin the Martyr and Clement of Alexandria believed that the stars were legitimate objects of worship for the "heathens" and this practice

---

[44] Rene Guenon, *Spiritual Authority and Temporal Power*, trans. Henry D. Fohr and Samuel D. Fohr (New York: Sophia Perennis, 1929), 65.

[45] William E. Dunstan, *Ancient Rome* (Blue Ridge Summit: Rowman & Littlefield Publishers, 2002), 467-8.

[46] Marian Hillar, *From Logos to Trinity: The Evolution of Religious Beliefs from Pythagoras to Tertullian* (Cambridge: Cambridge University Press, 2012), ix.

was seen as a middle point between heathenism and Christianity, and thus a more tolerable form of nature worship.[47]

Even though Bremmer agrees with Nock that the origins of Christianity have no relation to the Mysteries, she leaves some room for discussion. She states of Christian Gnostics:

> *There can indeed be little doubt that elements of the Mysteries had been appropriated by some Christian Gnostic groups... It is certainly the case that the word mystêrion in general has a cognitive content ('secret') rather than a ritual one in Gnostic writings, as is also the case in the writings of Mani, the founder of the only world religion that has become extinct. In various ways the Gnostics seem to have borrowed especially from the Orphics and the Orphic-Bacchic Mysteries, as scholars already began to note around 1900.*[48]

She goes on to state: "One thing, though, is clear from these examples from Justin, Tertullian and the Gnostics: pagans did see similarities between their Mysteries and the Christian sacraments, and some Christian groups were not averse to borrowing from the Mysteries."[49] Although

---

[47] Pike, *Morals and Dogma*, 511. In this passage, Pike is referring directly to "*Sabæans*."

[48] Bremmer, *Initiation,* 158-9.

[49] Bremmer, *Initiation,* 160.

many church Fathers preached against the Mysteries and some Roman rulers actively closed them, the church undoubtedly assimilated its language and notion of secrecy, leaving Bremmer to conclude "... in some way, those ancient Mysteries are still amongst us."[50]

Looking forward in history, we find by the 7th century that Eastern Christians had come to terms with the knowledge they inherited from the Mysteries. Aramaic Christians not only retained copies of ancient works, but they were actively engaged in the study of these works, continuing the intellectual traditions of the Mysteries under the Ḥanīf doctrine of Christianity. According to Gutas, Christian "high culture" was indifferent to so-called "pagan Greek learning." In places like Persia and Egypt, the Christians' main enemies were other sects of Christianity, primarily the Chalcedonian churches, who did not tolerate alternative Christian denominations that made a place for the knowledge of the Mysteries.[51] In the non-Chalcedonian Christian world, the educated class had embraced their intellectual heritage from the heyday of the Mysteries and reconciled it with Christianity. Yet, it was this reconciliation between Christianity and the Mysteries that placed a wedge between the Western and Eastern churches.

---

[50] Bremmer, *Initiation,* 163-4.

[51] Gutas, *Greek Thought, Arabic Culture*, 18.

Islam and the Mysteries

A variety of historical phenomena have stirred the curiosity of scholars and laymen alike concerning the early history of Islam, causing some to dismiss the dominant narrative about its origins. Chief among these is the case of Islam's written history within the first two centuries following its inception. Indeed, it appears that the intellectual renaissance in both religious and extra-religious sciences did not begin until the 9th and 10th centuries C.E., some 200 years after the advent of Islam. Though this fact is cause for speculation, it should not lead one to far out conspiracy theories and revisionist history like those once espoused by the likes of Patricia Crone, Michael Cook, and John Wansbrough.[52] Rather, this fact signifies the pivotal role Islam played at this critical juncture in Near Eastern history.

One of the best contextualizations of Islam does not come from a specialist in Islamic studies, but from a British journalist. In his book, *Catastrophe: An Investigation into the Origins of the Modern World*, David Keys underscores some key world events that took place between the 6th and 7th centuries C.E. One event was the 535 C.E. volcanic eruption between the current-day Indonesian islands of Java and Sumatra that had

---

[52] Patricia Crone and Michael Cook authored *Hagarism: The Making of the Islamic World* (Cambridge: Cambridge University Press, 1977) and John Wansbrough authored *Quranic Studies: Sources and Methods of Scriptural Interpretation*, London Oriental Series, v. 31 (Oxford: Oxford University Press, 1977), both of which cite the lack of early Arabic sources on Islam, hold a broad skepticism of early Islamic sources, and posit extreme alternative narratives to the dominant narrative on the origins of Islam.

global effects.[53] Another event was the outbreak of the Bubonic plague that entered the Roman Empire through Egypt and decimated much of its population. It eventually spread east to Persia and China.[54] At the same time, the Slavs, a coalition of warrior peoples from Eastern Europe and Central Asia, was attacking Rome from the north.[55]

These calamities – among other factors – destabilized the Roman Empire to the degree that the Persians overcome them and seized much of their territories. This political tenuity in the region set the stage for the expanding Islamic empire to inherit not only their lands, but also the intellectual heritage of these two major civilizations of the Near East. This intellectual heritage was primarily the efforts of scholars influenced by the ancient Egyptian, Greek, and Persian Mysteries. However, they lay dormant during the 6th and 7th centuries due to the turmoil. Keys even notes the dearth of writing worldwide during this period. Instead, many of the ancient manuscripts were preserved by Christian monks who lived on the outskirts of the Roman Empire, such as Syria, Persia, Upper Egypt, and North Africa. It is well-established that they were the primary conduits of ancient Sabian knowledge to Muslim civilization.

---

[53] David Keys, *Catastrophe: An Investigation into the Origins of the Modern World* (New York: Ballantine Books, 1999), 448.

[54] Keys, 31–47.

[55] Keys, 59–75.

These were works on philosophy, agriculture, and astronomy among other disciplines and this was the primary literature that was read in the Islamic world for its first two centuries. This fact is evidenced by Ibn al-Nadīm, who in his *al-Fihrist*, lists the books known to the Muslim world at the time. In addition to scholars and works within the Islamic canon, he also includes the works of previous religious groups, sects, and philosophers. These were original works from the original authors or those to whom the works were ascribed albeit in Arabic translation. This means that the fields of knowledge, debates, and positions of the ancients documented by Ibn al-Nadīm were being internationalized and made accessible to all who could read Arabic.

We commonly view the rise of Islam in the Near East as an external force originating with the Arabs who were cut off from all the religious, philosophical, and political turmoil in the region. Yet, an examination of early Islamic history in the full context of the Near East will reveal just how connected their histories were. And were we to consider the turmoil between the early Christians and the Mysteries, it is not unexpected that the early Muslims would address similar religious debates.

The history of Islam's contact with the Persian Mysteries begins with Alexander the Great's triumph over Persia. Ibn al-Nadīm relates a story verbatim from Abū Sahl ibn Nawbakht's inextant work, *al-Nahbuṭān* (*Two Things Seized Upon*).[56] Abū Sahl states that after Alexander invaded

---

[56] This is the translation of the title provided by Bayard Dodge. Abū al-Faraj Muḥammad ibn Isḥaq Ibn al-Nadīm, *The Fihrist of Al-Nadim: A Tenth Century*

Persia and killed Dārā the son of Dārā (Darius III), he destroyed buildings and erased the inscriptions so that the knowledge recorded therein could not be salvaged. Alexander then made copies of the books of astronomy, medicine, and astrology he found in the archives, translated them into Greek and Coptic, then burnt the Persian originals. Alexander then sent these spoils to the scholars of Egypt and Greece for them to interpret them and benefit their society. However, Abū Sahl states that Persian knowledge, which they inherited from the ancient Sabians of Babylon (i.e., the Chaldeans), was preserved by Zoroastrians in India and China. The next Persian ruler, Ardashīr sent for these works to make copies from them and restore the ancient knowledge to Persia. Sabūr, the son of Ardashīr, continued this initiative, compiling these works, he says, in the same manner they were transmitted from Babylon.[57]

Abū Sahl's story suggests that the fierce conflict between Rome and Persia was not confined to political and military dominance, but access to knowledge as well. The Romans defeated the Persians with their might and sought to incapacitate them by dispossessing them of their knowledge. Notably, Alexander's translation project alludes to the fact that the language in which ideas was recorded and discussed was also key to the power play. It allowed Alexander to claim this knowledge for the

---

Survey of Muslim Culture, trans. Bayard Dodge, vol. 2 (New York: Columbia University Press, 1970), 572.

[57] Ibn Nadīm, *Al-Fihrist*, 334 and Gutas, *Greek Thought, Arabic Culture*, 39-40.

Greeks without attribution to the Persians, effectively wiping out their history.

Nevertheless, the Persians were able to reconstruct their intellectual tradition through Persian copies of books stored on the peripheries of their land. The claiming or restoration of an intellectual tradition is not an overnight process. It would have taken generations of scholars to translate, comprehend, and record existing information simply to reach their previous level of knowledge, let alone build upon it.

The Persian ruler, Chosroes I (531-578 C.E.) and his grandson Chosroes II (570-628 C.E.), also continued the efforts to reestablish the Persian Mystery Schools. Chosroes I was known as a man of erudition and intellectual curiosity. Though he was a Zoroastrian, he welcomed the Christians who were persecuted in by the Byzantines and listened to the Christians' theological debates. Chosroes II reigned during the lifetime of the Prophet Muhammad and was one of the rulers who received a letter from the Prophet. Upon receiving the letter, Chosroes II became incensed and shredded the letter. When the Prophet Muhammad heard of the ruler's response, he petitioned God in prayer to remove his kingdom from him in the same manner. Within years the Romans had reclaimed the lands that Persia had taken following the death of Emperor Maurice and soon after the Muslims had conquered what remained of the Persian Empire.

The Roman Emperor Heraclius would also respond violently, and their land would eventually be conquered by the Muslims as well.[58]

To make this timeline of events clear, we must remember that Justinian, who led the conversion and expelling of the Neo-Platonist Mysteries ruled from 527 C.E. until his death in 565 C.E. Chosroes I ruled from 531 C.E. until his death in 579 C.E. The Prophet Muhammad was born around 570 C.E. and he was roughly the same age as Chosroes II and the Roman Emperor Heraclius. Emperor Maurice's execution took place in 602 C.E. prior to the start of Muhammad's prophetic mission. So, Maurice's persecution of Ḥarrānian Sabians would have occurred during Muhammad's lifetime, just as the divisions in Christianity solidified and the Persians were rebuilding their academy and Mystery Schools. Adamant "pagans," which to Christians included Neo-Platonists, Gnostics, Magians, and polytheistic cults, would have found a home in the deserts of the Hijaz prior to Islam. Yet, the Qur'an made it clear that polytheism and certain pagan and magical rituals were unacceptable forms of belief and spiritual practice. The Sabians mentioned in the Qur'an would have been among these above-mentioned groups. More specifically, they would have been among the myriad of syncretic religious groups in the Near East, that mixed Judaism with Magianism, as suggested by al-Bīrūnī,[59] or Jewish-Christian Gnosticism, as suggested

---

[58] John A. Morrow, *The Covenants of the Prophet Muhammad with the Christians of the World* (Kettering, Ohio: Angelico Press, Sophia Perennis, 2013), 49.

[59] Muḥammad ibn Aḥmad Bīrūnī and Eduard Sachau, *The Chronology of Ancient Nations: An English Version of the Arabic Text of the Athâr-Ul-Bâkiya of*

by Van Bladel,[60] or any other religiously hybrid sect that flourished in the Near East throughout the 6th and 7th centuries.

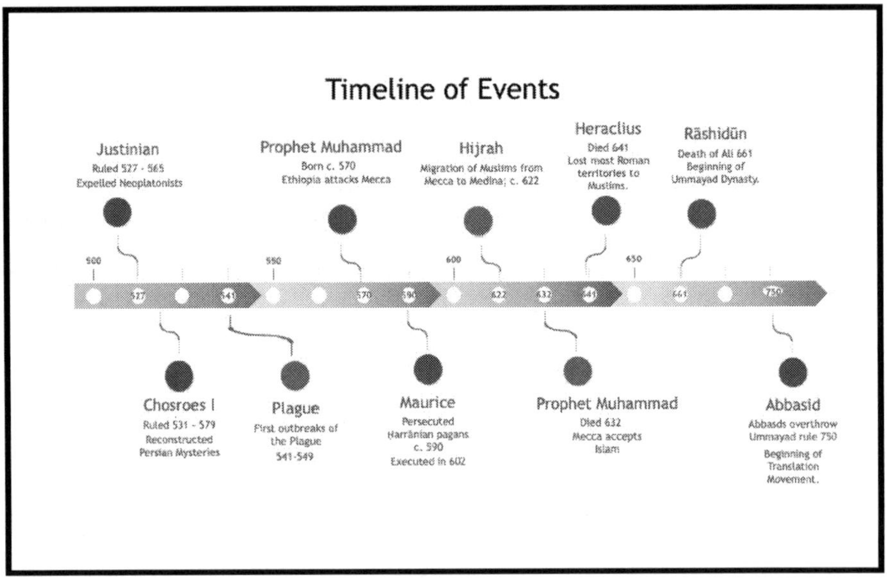

Muslims would later negotiate the veracity and utility of philosophy and other ancient sciences. These negotiations emerged during the Abbasid

---

Albîrûnî, or, "Vestiges of the Past" (London: Oriental Translation Fund of Great Britain and Ireland, 1879), 188.

60 Kevin Thomas Van Bladel, *From Sasanian Mandaeans to Ṣābians of the Marshes*, Leiden Studies in Islam and Society, volume 6 (Boston: Brill, 2017), 98.

era, 750-1258 C.E., when caliphs like al-Manṣūr, Hārūn al-Rashīd, and al-Ma'mūn sponsored the translation of ancient philosophical, scientific, religious, and literary texts that were preserved in the region in Greek, Syriac, Persian, and Sanskrit into Arabic. Therefore, when early Arab Muslims entered the imperial scene, they encountered societies with vibrant intellectual cultures that had suffered from religious fragmentation and syncretism. Gutas notes, "As for the Arab Muslims… they viewed the study of all the sciences as a continuation of the indigenous tradition as well as of the policies of glorious emperors of previous ages…"[61] Undoubtedly, Muslims continued the reestablishment of the Persian Mysteries, but under the Ḥanīf doctrine of Islam. In many ways, the situation was ideal for the burgeoning Islamic empire. After its incubation period in the Arabian Peninsula, we find that its imperial efforts often preceded its proselytizing efforts. Islam would nevertheless prevail in these lands as the answer to the questions of the age but not without succumbing to the same controversies.

While a more extensive study is forthcoming, it appears that traditional-minded Muslims argued the same theological positions as the early Christian theologians. One cannot help but notice the parallels between the positions of the Jewish theologian Philo,[62] Christian theologian

---

[61] Gutas, *Greek Thought, Arabic Culture*, 43.

[62] Marian Hillar, *From Logos to Trinity: The Evolution of Religious Beliefs from Pythagoras to Tertullian* (Cambridge: Cambridge University Press, 2012), 53.

Origen,[63] and Muslim theologian al-Ghazalī,[64] who argued for the creation of the universe against their interlocutors who considered the universe eternal and uncreated. Perhaps this argument culminated in Islam with Ibn Rushd's retort to al-Ghazālī in *Tahāfut al-Tahāfut* in which the crux of his position was to state that the "craft of *ḥikmah*" (i.e., philosophy and metaphysical knowledge) should be transmitted like other crafts.[65] Though Ibn Rushd's argument was largely rejected by the Muslim world in favor of al-Ghazālī's explicit Ḥanīf stance, the works of Ibn Rushd, Ibn Sīnā, al-Farābī, and other Sabian-leaning Muslim scholars would be the foundations of Western Europe's Enlightenment. Thus, demonstrating James' point that the North African inheritors of knowledge from the Mysteries would be responsible for passing the "crafts" (i.e., the Mysteries) to Western civilization.

---

[63] Origen, *On First Principles*, trans. John Behr, vol. 1, 2 vols. (Oxford: Oxford University Press, 2017), 153.

[64] Abu Hamid Ghazālī, *Al-Ghazali's Tahāfut al-Falāsifah: Incoherence of the Philosophers*, trans. Sabih Ahmad Kamali, Pakistan Philosophical Congress Publication, no. 3 (Lahore: Pakistan Philosophical Congress, 1963), 6.

[65] Averroës, *The Attitude of Islam Towards Science and Philosophy: A Translation of Ibn Rushd's (Averroës) Famous Treatise Faṣlul-al-Maqāl*, trans. Aadil Amin Kak (Sarup & Sons, 2003), 139.

CHAPTER THREE
The Mystery Milieu

“

إِنَّ الَّذِينَ آمَنُوا وَالَّذِينَ هَادُوا وَالصَّابِئِينَ وَالنَّصَارَىٰ وَالْمَجُوسَ
وَالَّذِينَ أَشْرَكُوا إِنَّ اللَّهَ يَفْصِلُ بَيْنَهُمْ يَوْمَ الْقِيَامَةِ إِنَّ اللَّهَ عَلَىٰ كُلِّ
شَيْءٍ شَهِيدٌ

It is those who believe, who claim to be Jews, the Sabians, the Christians, the Magians, and those who divide the attributes of God (into various deities) that indeed God will adjudicate between on the Day of Resurrection. It is God who is a Witness over everything.
(al-Ḥajj: 17)

The period between the rise of Christianity until the rise of Islam was characterized by an intellectual fervor in the greater Near East that spilled over into the realm of political and religious factionalism. For ideas to survive in such an environment, the faithful had to fight for their beliefs with the word and the sword. In the case of the Roman-Persian conflict, fighting was about access to knowledge as much as it was about land and power. If we contemplate this point, we will find that knowledge, more than anything, is the backbone of civilization. For a civilization to prosper, it needs free and unfettered access to knowledge for building, medicine, warfare, etc. Yet, the knowledge of concern was not only material in nature, but metaphysical as well.

While the environment was extremely hostile for adherents of the Mysteries in the Roman heartland between the 5th and 6th centuries C.E., the Mysteries persisted on the outskirts of the Roman provinces. George G. M. James notes that edicts targeting followers of the Mysteries issued by Theodosius and later by Justinian in the 6th century caused them to flee to "adjacent lands in Africa, Arabia and Asia Minor." He states that they would preserve the teachings of the Mysteries in the Arabic language as "Moors," i.e., Islamic civilization.[66] The two main groups that fit this description are the Ḥarrānians and the Mandaeans, two groups who Muslim scholars have historically referred to as Sabians and themselves taken on this designation.

In this chapter, I will examine details surrounding the Ḥarrānians, Ḥanīfs, Mandaeans, Naṣoraeans, Arab Naṣārā and Yahūd, as well as the ancient Egyptians, and Majūs (Magians). The Mandaeans are known to have constructed their religion around a secret group of scholars known as the *Nāsurati* or Nāṣoraeans. Additionally, we know from Arabic sources that the ancient Egyptian religion was considered Ṣabianism and it had similar beliefs and practices to the Ḥarrānian and Mandaean religions, as well as the ancient Mystery Schools, as believed by James, Freemasonic,

---

[66] James, *Stolen Legacy*, 31-2.

Theosophic, and some academic authors. Finally, I will focus on the relationship between the Majūs and Zoroastrianism with Sabianism.

Ḥarrānians

The Sabians of Ḥarrān, as they were penned in Arabic sources, were known in Latin as *Carrhae*. They were primarily located in Asia Minor on the southern tip of present-day Turkey. They must be one of the displaced groups of the Mysteries James alluded to in *Stolen Legacy*. De Blois and Michel Tardieu attempt to draw a distinction between Gnosticism and "pagan" religion. They contend that the Sabians of the Qur'an was a Gnostic group, while the Ḥarrānians were simply adherents to a pagan religion. However, these notions are not mutually exclusive given early Christian writings that described their metaphysical foes as pagans, whether they were sophisticated Gnostics or unlettered agriculturalists. And as keepers of ancient knowledge from Egypt and beyond, the Ḥarrānian Sabians fit James' description perfectly.

We should note that the Ḥarrānians accepted the Sabian label by the reign of al-Muʿtaḍid in the late 9th century. From the literature, we can conclude that they knew Arabic and Islamic scripture well enough to understand what was implied by the word. Most Western scholars insinuate that classical Muslim scholars forgot the true identity of the Sabians in the Qur'an by the time the Abbasid Caliph al-Ma'mūn encountered them in Ḥarrān.[67] Those Western scholars believe that the Muslims gullibly

[67] In the account reported by Ibn al-Nadīm, al-Ma'mūn passed through Ḥarrān on his way to fight the Byzantines. Noting their strange appearance, he inquired into

accepted the Ḥarrānians' self-identification as Sabians, which gave them a *dhimmi* status. However, it is unlikely that Ibn al-Nadīm's account happened exactly as it was reported. Al-Ma'mūn was a patron of the translation of ancient Sabian knowledge to Arabic, having found the famed House of Wisdom (*Bayt al-Ḥikmah*). The Ḥarrānians were among the most prominent beneficiaries of this patronage during the Abbasid era, so it is doubtful that al-Ma'mūn adopted such a puritanical attitude toward them, especially since he led an Inquisition (*Miḥnah*) against the Hadith scholar, Aḥmad ibn Ḥanbal, over the use of reason and ancient knowledge. The story is simply an attempt to explain the fact that the Ḥarrānians identified as Sabians.

Beyond self-identification, there are historical connections between the Mystery Schools and the Ḥarrānians. After Justinian exiled the Neoplatonists from Athens in 529 C.E.,[68] they passed through Ḥarrān on their way to seek refuge in Persia. The native Ḥarrānians then invited those exiled Neoplatonists to be their leaders. Stroumsa accepts this line

---

what type of *dhimmi* they were. They did not reply immediately, so al-Ma'mūn gave them until his return to become Muslims, Jews, or Christians, or face execution. Many converted to either Islam or Christianity. Those who chose not to convert devised to call themselves Sabians. Abū al-Faraj Muḥammad ibn Isḥaq Ibn Nadīm, *Al-Fihrist* (Beirut: Dar al-Ma'rifah, 937), 445–46. Khazʿal al-Mājidī rightly points out that this story is only related by Ibn al-Nadīm on the authority of a Christian, and is not corroborated by other reports, Khazʿal al-Mājidī, *Al-Mithūlūjīyah al-Mandā'īyah* (Damascus: Dār al-Nīnawā, 2010), 28.

[68] William E. Dunstan, *Ancient Rome* (Blue Ridge Summit: Rowman & Littlefield Publishers, 2002), 526.

of thinking, but states that the data is not conclusive enough to draw a detailed picture on the nature of this relationship. However, there is more evidence to suggest a strong Neoplatonist influence in Ḥarrān. As late as 590 C.E., the Emperor Maurice ordered the persecution of Ḥarranian "pagans."[69]

Additionally, Tamara Green establishes a deeper historical relationship between Arabs and the city of Ḥarrān throughout Antiquity. As early as 132 BCE, both Arabic and Aramaic names were found in the royal register. She suggests that the Arameans encouraged their rule over the city and that they were given control over the trade routes that passed through this region. She also evidences the roaming of Arab tribes in the northern Mesopotamia region near Ḥarrān as early as the 4th century. She states that some Arabs ruled neighboring Edessa shortly before that date.

Recounting Ḥarrān and Edessa's role in the religious conflicts of the 6th century, Green points out that the Arabs of the Lakhmid kingdom of Ḥīrā were loyal to Persia, who accepted the doctrine of the Monophysites. King Nuʿmān II of Ḥīrā did the bidding of the Persian king, Khawad, by attacking Ḥarrān and Edessa in the late 6th century. The Persians attempted to take Ḥarrān and Edessa on several occasions unsuccessfully. Later under Chosroes I, Edessa was able to claim immunity from the

---

[69] Sarah Stroumsa, *Maimonides in His World: Portrait of a Mediterranean Thinker*, Jews, Christians, and Muslims from the Ancient to the Modern World (Princeton, N.J: Princeton University Press, 2009), 89, and David Pingree, "The Sābians of Harrān and the Classical Tradition," *International Journal of the Classical Tradition* 9, no. 1 (June 1, 2002): 8–35, 16-20

Persians because it was largely Christian, while Ḥarrān was not provided immunity on the grounds that, "…most of them are not Christians but are of the old faith."[70]

This history shows us that the Arabs have a long relationship with the city of Ḥarrān and its surrounding areas that was still in effect in the 6th century just prior to the rise of Islam. They ruled, dominated trade, sometimes defended, and other times attacked the city. Throughout Christian Byzantine suppression, Persian attacks, an epidemic, and natural disasters, Ḥarrān remained loyal to the so-called "old faith" of Sabianism and they would remain on this faith well into Islamic rule.

The Ḥarrānian religion is reported to share characteristics with the Mysteries in that they consisted of planet worship and ritual sacrifice. Ibn al-Nadīm described their rituals as *asrār* (mysteries) that take place at one *bayt* (shrine) or another. In Bayard Dodge's translation of the Sabian initiation account from *al-Fihrist*, he translates *asrār* as mysteries, and even draws parallels between their initiation and the Mithraic Mysteries. In their ceremonies they repeat the phrase, "our Lord is the victor, to whom we give delight."[71] Dodge mentions that this could be an allusion

---

[70] Tamara M. Green, *The City of the Moon God: Religious Traditions of Harran*, Religions in the Graeco-Roman World, 0927-7633, v. 114 (Leiden: E.J. Brill, 1992), 46–53.

[71] Ibn al-Nadīm, *The Fihrst*, 771. The statement given in Arabic is *rabbunā al-qāhir wa naḥnu nasurruhu*. This may also be an allusion to the word, Nāṣoraean, which we will cover in its place, Ibn Nadīm, *Al-Fihrist*, 455.

to the deity Mithras, who was known as "the victor" or "the invincible."[72] According to Ibn al-Nadīm's description of their cultic practices and Dodge's astute observation, I see ample reason to associate the Sabians of Ḥarrān continued the rites of the Ancient Mystery Schools. They had festivals dedicated to astral deities as well as an intellectual strain that studied the works of the ancient Greeks.[73] They considered Hermes to be their prophet[74] and adopted the identity of Sabians as evidenced by the narration of their encounter with the Caliph al-Ma'mūn.

Thābit ibn Qurrah (d. 901 C.E.) was the most famous of these Ḥarrānian pagans, who was a mathematician and translator of Greek and Syriac texts into Arabic. Throughout the 10th century C.E., many of Thābit's descendants held rank in Baghdad's intelligentsia, even while preserving their ancient religion, dubbed *ḥanputā* (a cognate to *ḥanīf*) by Thābit himself. In Syriac, *ḥanputā* means "pagan foe."[75] However, for a Muslim

---

[72] Ibn al-Nadīm, *The Fihrst*, 770.

[73] Pingree, "Sābians of Harrān," 18.

[74] The *interpretatio* of Herodotus found Hermes to be analogous to the Egyptian god, Thoth, who was the master of wisdom, author of the alphabet, and tongue of the creator god Ptah. In the Mesopotamian pantheon, Hermes was analogous to the moon god, Sīn, and Nebo, the scribal deity; Green, *The City of the Moon God*, 85–86.

[75] Kevin Thomas Van Bladel, *The Arabic Hermes: From Pagan Sage to Prophet of Science*, Oxford Studies in Late Antiquity (Oxford: Oxford University Press, 2009), 64-6. In modern vernacular, the term *ḥanputā* might translate to the epithet "heathen."

audience, this word would mean the monotheistic strand of the religion. It was only the Arabic of the Qur'an that converted the word Ḥanīf to a positive meaning. Prior to Islam, Syriac Christians apparently understood *ḥanputā* to mean pagan. We see the evidence for this in Gregory Bar Hebraeus' (known in Arabic sources as Abū al-Faraj ibn Hārūn) transmission of the words of Thābit ibn Qurrah in which he claims that the Sabians of Ḥarrān are the inheritors of the *ḥanputā* or Ḥanīfs. Thābit, who was a master of the Arabic language and the Islamic sciences despite hailing from a Sabian lineage, attempted to invert the meaning of the word by claiming Ḥanīfīyah for the Ḥarrānian religion.

We have already witnessed in the story of Abraham how a look into the Sabian narrative adds another dimension to our understanding of the word Ḥanīf as used in the Qur'an, as well as the main lines of division in the among ancient religious sects. In the next section, we will find that one needs to look no farther than the Mandaeans – one of the prime groups Muslim scholars identify as Sabians – to uncover examples of counternarratives to major Biblical and Qur'anic accounts.

Mandaeans

The Mandaeans are an ethno-religious gnostic[76] group primarily situated in Southern Iraq and Iran. They are known in the Iraqi society as *Ṣubba*,

---

[76] Buckley says that gnosis is the best translation of the Mandaean religion. *Mandā* means "to know." They are the last surviving gnostics, which have been overshadowed by orthodox forms of Christianity (or Judaism). Then she surmises what Muslim jurists had determined over a millenium prior, "They defy

a local adaptation of the word Sabian. Kevin van Bladel characterizes them as an insulated community, who practice endogamy and often live in backwater villages and the marshlands. He believes that their pre-modern history is likely to remain obscure. Still, he argues that their origins as a religion date back to the 5th century C.E. under Sassanian hegemony.[77] Jorunn Jacobsen Buckley believes that the Mandaeans were originally from the Jordan – Palestine region. They later migrated to Ḥarrān before eventually settling in Iraq – Iran. This appears to corroborate the idea that the exiled followers of the Mystery Schools stopped at Ḥarrān on their way to Persia; perhaps some settled in Ḥarrān and others continued to Persia, which was far more open to the teachings of the Mysteries. Edwin Yamauchi believes that their origins were in ancient Babylon, but Rudolf Macuch categorically rejects this opinion.[78] The Iraqi historian, Khazʿal al-Mājidī, believes that their origins as a religion go back to the 5th century B.C.E. in Mesopotamia. According to al-Mājidī, they also had extended stays in many of the major centers of the Near East such as Egypt, Ḥarrān, Jerusalem, and Persia.[79] ʿAbdullah

---

easy categorization. Neither Jewish, Christian, nor recognizably 'pagan…'" *The Mandaeans*, 7.

[77] Kevin Thomas Van Bladel, *From Sasanian Mandaeans to Ṣābians of the Marshes*, vol. 6, Leiden Studies in Islam and Society (Boston: Brill, 2017), 3, 5.

[78] Jorunn Jacobsen Buckley, *The Mandaeans: Ancient Texts and Modern People*, American Academy of Religion the Religions Series (New York: Oxford University Press, 2002), 3-4.

[79] Khazʿal al-Mājidī, *Al-Mithūlūjīyah al-Mandāʾīyah* (Damascus: Dār al-Nīnawā, 2010), 31.

Samak believes the most correct opinion is that their origins are from Babylon, in current-day Iraq then it spread to other civilizations like Egypt, the Levant, India, Greece, Persia, and the Arabian Peninsula.[80]

Their history is clearly intertwined with that of the Ḥarrānians as well as the Jews, Christians, and even the ancient Akkadians. Their folklore is full of references to these peoples and E.S. Drower and al-Mājidī have found elements of Akkadian rites in their rituals. Most Western scholars of the Mandaeans (and al-Mājidī) insist on separating their history from that of the Ḥarrānians, but when including narratives from the Mandaeans, must relate stories that confirm their connections to the Ḥarrānians. For instance, one of their scriptures is called *Haran Gawaita* (*H'r'n G'w'yt'*), meaning "the Interior of Ḥarrān," named for the fact that the residents of Ḥarrān gave them refuge from the Jewish Chaldaeans. Again, this supports the idea that Ḥarrān was a safe haven for non-Abrahamic elements in the region. Al-Bīrūnī supports this notion as well, as he believes that the Ḥarrānians used Abraham's stay in Ḥarrān against him by saying he attracted leprosy there; a narrative that also appears in Mandaean literature.[81] Likewise, when Drower relates the story of Dana Nuk's journey to the 7th heaven, she states that this most learned of the first *Nāṣurati* (Nāṣoraean) scholars was inspired by God to take on

---

[80] Samak, *Al-Ṣābi'ūn*, 40.

[81] Tamara M. Green, *The City of the Moon God: Religious Traditions of Harran*. Religions in the Graeco-Roman World, vol. 114. (Leiden: Brill, 1992), 15.

another way (*ṭarīqah*), which was the way of *Sīn*, the moon god, said to be worshiped by the Ḥarrānians.[82] Moreover, the Mandaeans also use the incident of the Caliph al-Ma'mūn in Ḥarrān as precedence for their Sabian status.[83]

Even though the Mandaeans appear to be a distinct group from the Ḥarrānians, we cannot deny the historical relationship However, to delve deeper into their connection with the greater Near East, we have to first discuss their class of priests and scholars, known as *Nāṣurati* or Nāṣoraeans.

Nāṣoraeans

The Iraqi historian, Khazʿal l-Mājidī, believes the origins of the Nāṣoraeans goes back to the Copper Age, around the 5th millennium B.C.E. somewhere between the Nile and Euphrates. They initially worshiped the water god named *Iyā*, which the Sumerians called *Enki*. The word, *Nāṣurati*, is said to mean "to notice" while some say it means "to chant" like a bird or in some unknown tongue. Al-Mājidī adds that the

---

[82] Dana Nuk was a member of the Nāṣurati during the time of Adam, when there was no other religion beside Mandā'ī. This supports the notion of the widespread belief that the original religion was one, but there were different expressions of it, as indicated by the word *ṭarīqah*. Moreover, they do not find a contradiction between a belief in a single Creator and worship through a celestial body such as the moon, Drower and Buckley, *Mandaeans of Iraq*, 6, 301, *cf* Ibn al-Nadīm's reports of the Ḥarrānian Sabian rituals involving *Sīn*, *The Fihrst*, vol. 2, 757, 764.

[83] Buckley, *The Mandaeans,* 5.

Syriac word is a cognate of the Arabic word, *naẓara*, making the meaning of the term "the Watchers."[84] So, Nāṣoraeans can be considered "those who watch the stars."[85]

Drower obviously sees Mandaeaism as a Mystery School, which features the Lesser Mysteries, made up of "ignorant or semi-ignorant laity," who are called Mandaeans, and the Greater Mysteries, made up of priests and scholars, referred to as Nāṣoraeans. A Nāṣoraean is one who possesses knowledge of the secret doctrine and constantly maintains ritual purity. When learning that some secret scrolls fell into Drower's hands – an uninitiated outsider – the Nāṣoraean priests threatened the guilty parties with punishment "in *this* world and the next" (Drower's emphasis), as is the case in many secret societies. Additionally, they also hate Jews and Jesus Christ, whose name they qualify with the descriptors "false" and "lying."[86] The nature of their hatred complicates matters for those researching their origins.

Based on documentary evidence dating back to the 5th century C.E. or prior, van Bladel and his predecessors believe that Mandaeism evolved

---

[84] Mājidī, *Al-Mandā'īyah*, 31.

[85] A note in which Drower discusses the classifications of angelic beings (the *uthri*, *natri*, and *melki*), she defines them as "the watchers in the sky." This could align with their dualist principles. The Nāṣoraeans could be the representations of the angels on earth. E. S. Drower, *The Secret Adam. A Study of Nasoraean Gnosis* (London: Oxford University Press, 1960), 330.

[86] Drower and Buckley, *Mandaeans of Iraq*, ix-xi.

out of a pre-existing "Jewish-Christian Mandaeism" known as Nāṣoraeanism. Naturally, van Bladel, like de Blois, searched for links to one of the early Gnostic Christian sects, noting that some early Syriac texts referred to Christians as *Nāṣrāyā*. The Eastern Church later employed the term *Kristyānā* to distinguish themselves from other denominations. Yet, the most puzzling question in making this connection is: how do Aramaic-speaking followers of Jesus of Nazareth (supposedly the origin of the word Nāṣoraean) transform into those who accuse their founder of being an evil demon and his followers as impure?

Van Bladel believes that the Nāṣoraeans started as Christians who criticized the beliefs and practices of other Christians. Then they later formulated their own separate religion, ripe with its own set of rituals and doctrines, which greatly depart from Christian orthodoxy. Not only that but the Nāṣoraeans also regard Christians as ignorant and unclean. Van Bladel then states that the Nāṣoraeans and Christians are analogous to Manichaeans and other Near Eastern religions; as well as Ismāʿīlīsm and Islam.[87] The problem with this analogy is that neither the Manichaeans or the Ismāʿīlīs were guilty of accusing any of their founders as being evil and corrupted.

I do not think this conundrum can be solved without changing our paradigm just a little. So, let us examine a new hypothesis that I propose

---

[87] Kevin Thomas Van Bladel, *From Sasanian Mandaeans to Ṣābians of the Marshes*, vol. 6, Leiden Studies in Islam and Society (Boston: Brill, 2017), 89-97.

below. I start with the premise that the word Nāṣoraean is a cognate for the Qur'anic term for Christians *Naṣārā* (singular *Naṣrānī*). Conforming to the view that pre-Islamic Arabia was infused with various types of Sabians, what if we suppose that the *Naṣārā* and "those who had become Jews"[88] addressed in the Qur'an were these Nāṣoraean remnants of the Mysteries, who were being expelled from Rome and suppressed in Ḥarrān less than a century prior? Perhaps, they were Neoplatonists, who could speak the language of the Jews and Christians but secretly held on to the ways of the Mystery Schools.

Let us also briefly deconstruct our common conception of the *Naṣārā* in the Qur'an. It is believed that the word, *Naṣrānī* is related to the city of Nazareth, which is the birthplace of Jesus. However, Arabic language scholars say this as a weak opinion because the relative adjective (*nisbah*) rarely takes this form.[89] In Western literature, de Blois and Carl Brockelman have both acknowledged this fact.[90] Still, the controversial Iraqi author, Faḍil al-Rabīʿī argues against this common conception because everyone from the city of Nazareth could be called *Naṣrānī*

---

[88] In the three verses that list Jews and Christians along with the *Ṣābi'ūn* (*al-Baqarah*: 62, *al-Mā'idah*: 69, and *al-Ḥajj:* 17) it refers to "those who had become Jews" (الذين هادوا *alladhīna hādū*). The Mandaeans claim to have become Jews at one point in their history, but then parted ways with them due to their execution of 360 Nāṣoraeans in Jerusalem, Mājidī, *Al-Mandā'īyah*, 40, and Buckley, *The Mandaeans*, 4.

[89] Muhammad Ibn Manẓūr, *Lisān al-ʿArab*, vol. 5 (Beirut: Dār Ṣādir, 1300), 211.

[90] Blois, "Naṣrānī and Ḥanīf," 11.

regardless of their religious affiliation, and this is usually not the case. Instead, he believes *Naṣārā* is derived from the word *anṣar*, meaning uncircumcised, revealing a key difference between the Jews and Sabians, who deem it impure to undergo circumcision.[91] Al-Rabīʿī argues that the *Naṣārā* were a type of *Ḥanīf* and were distinct from the philosophically inspired *Masīḥīyyīn*. He is correct about the association between *Ḥanīfs* and *Naṣārā* in the Ḥijāz. Waraqah ibn Nawfal, Qays ibn Sa'idah al-Ayadi, 'Uthman ibn al-Huwayrith, and Abu Amir the Monk were all Christians listed among the *Ḥanīfs*.[92] He is also correct that the Qur'an never addresses Christians as *Masīḥīyyīn*, only *Naṣārā*. Likewise, Muslim historians usually categorize Arab *Naṣārā* prior to Islam among the *Ḥanīfs*. However, my assessment is that his distinction between *Naṣārā* and *Masīḥīyyīn* constitutes an inversion of religious personalities, stories, symbols, and language. It is similar to the inversion of meanings for Semitic cognates to the word *ḥanīf*.

Renè Guenon posits that inversion in this sense relies on the principle of duality (which the Nāṣoraeans are fully acquainted with). It occurs when

---

[91] Fāḍil al-Rabīʿī, *Al-Masīḥ al-ʿArabī: Al-Naṣrānīyyah Fī al-Jazīrah al-ʿArabīyyah Wa al-Ṣirā' al-Bīzanṭī al-Fārisī* (Beirut: Riad El-Rayyes Books, 2009), 28-9. Al-Rabīʿī references the hadith لا يؤمنكم أنصَر ولا أزَن ولا أفرَع "Let not an uncircumcised man lead you, nor one who holds his bladder or one who is habitually delusional." Additionally, al-Rabīʿī does not believe Jesus was born in Nazareth in current-day Palestine, as is characteristic of his school of Biblical scholarship.

[92] Jawwād ʿAlī, *Al-Mufaṣṣal Fī Tārīkh al-ʿArab Qabl al-Islām*, 3rd ed., vol. 6. (Baghdad: University of Baghdad, 1947), 457-61.

one religious institution takes on the religious personalities, stories, symbols, and language of another and attributes orthodoxy to itself. Surely, this might be the most common form of *interpretatio* and source of religious confusion in the world, which allows some groups to benefit in secret at the expense of others. Guenon says: " This is really the whole secret of certain campaigns… it sometimes so happens that people who imagine that they are fighting the devil, whatever their particular notion of the devil may be, are thus turned, without the least suspicion of the fact on their part, into his best servants!"[93] Considering these inversions and the minority status of Christians in the Ḥijāz, it is possible that the term *Naṣārā* in the Qur'an was a term used for multiple syncretic sects or individuals in the Ḥijāz who philosophized on the nature of Christ such as Neoplatonists, Elchasaites, and Naṣoraeans.

Arab Naṣārā and Yahūd

From an historical perspective, we know that Arabs along the peripheries of Byzantium and Persia embraced Christianity prior to Islam. The son of the first Ghassanid king, al-Ḥārith (528-569 C.E.) – sometimes called al-Ḥārith ibn Abī Shumr – played an important role in helping the Roman emperor, Justinian (an opponent of the Mystery Schools), fight the Persians and Arabs of Iraq. The Byzantines later gave al-Ḥārith the titles, phylarch (tribe leader) and *al-Biṭrīq* (general; the highest title after king).

---

[93] Rene Guenon, *The Reign of Quantity and the Signs of the Times*, trans. Lord Northbourne (New York: Sophia Perennis, 1945), 202-7.

The Ghassanids officially embraced the Monophysite Church of Syria in the 4th century C.E. Upon visiting Constantinople, al-Ḥārith was able to convince the authorities to name an Arab of his tribe as a Bishop despite their theological differences.[94]

To the east in Mesopotamia, the Lakhmid city of al-Ḥīra was home to a population of *ʿIbbādī Naṣārā*. While the Lakhmids were Arab *Naṣārā* heavily influenced by Hellenistic (i.e., pagan) culture, they intermingled with Persians, Akkadians, and Armenians. They rivaled the Ghassanids and enjoyed the patronage of the Sassanids.[95] Christianity entered Yemen through various channels. It arrived from the Levant, the Ḥijāz, then Yemen, as well as from Iraq by way of trade caravans. Greek and Roman sailors also acquainted Yemenis with the religion, as well as the Ethiopians, who officially accepted Christianity in the 4th century C.E.[96] As the history goes, the Jewish Yemeni king, Dhū Nuwās, was persecuting the *Naṣārā* of Najrān. The Ethiopian kingdom of Axum came to their rescue either at the behest of a man named Dhū Thaʾlabān or from Justinian himself. This rescue mission was followed by the Axumite occupation in the Southern Arabian Peninsula, in which Abraha al-

---

[94] Shawqi Ḍayf, *Al-ʿAṣr al-Jāhilī*, 11th ed., vol. 1, Tarikh Al-Adab al-'Arabi (Cairo: Dār al-Ma'ārif, 1960), 41.

[95] Ḍayf, Al-ʿAṣr al-Jāhilī, 47.

[96] Jurji Zaydan, *Al-ʿArab Qabl al-Islām*, 3rd ed. (Cairo: Dar al-Hilal, 1922), 126.

Ashram was placed as general.[97] He would later lead the attack on the Ka'bah alluded to in *al-Fīl*:1-5 and expounded upon in *sīrah* and *tafsīr* literature.

Clearly, through these examples, we see the degree to which Christianity influenced the major kingdoms and urban centers of the Arabian Peninsula. Their involvement in both religious and political affairs had significant effects on the neighboring empires. But what about the interior of Arabia? Although sources name specific Christians from the Ḥijāz, Ghada Osman believes that there was no full-blown Christian community to speak of. Conversion to Christianity was done on an individual basis by truth-seekers or Ḥanīfs,[98] who other Semitic speakers would have considered pagans. Their lack of community was because Christianity was then new to the cities of Arabia in the 6th century. Their isolation and few numbers kept them from forming a church. And since we know very little about their creed, it could be the case that they all had different understandings of Christianity.[99] Given what we know of the political turbulence of the time, we should understand that the emperors of Byzantium saw all Christians outside of their domain or unaligned with them politically as covert followers of the Mystery Schools, who fled

---

[97] Jonathan Porter Berkey, *The Formation of Islam: Religion and Society in the Near East, 600-1800*, Themes in Islamic History 2 (New York: Cambridge University Press, 2003), 47 and Zaydan, *Al-'Arab*, 124.

[98] Osman, "Pre-Islamic Arab Converts," 68.

[99] Osman, "Pre-Islamic Arab Converts," 75.

Rome to seek refuge in Persia, the interior of Arabia, or the interior of Africa.

Mecca

By the 6th century, Mecca had developed into a commercial and pagan religious center in the Ḥijāz. It was originally populated by the Jurham tribe, a remnant of the extinct Arab tribes that welcomed Abraham's wife, Hagar, and son, Ishmael. Later Yemeni tribes began to migrate to the area, among them the Khuzā'ah, the tribe of ʿAmr ibn Luḥay, who is credited with introducing the worship of idols at the Kaʿbah.[100] In the mid-5th century C.E., historians believe that the tribe of Quraysh drove out the Khuzā'ah and assumed prominence in Mecca. There is no consensus on the origins of the Quraysh tribe. Shawqī Ḍayf postulates that they were of Nabatean origin who retreated south from their battles with Rome or were originally from the Najd region. If they were "pagans" fighting against the Romans, then it is possible that they were followers of the Mystery Schools who were ousted at the turn of the 5th century. Whatever their origins, it appears that they initially allied with the Christian Abyssinians against Yemen, but later switched their loyalties. This earned them the angst of the Abyssinians, who attempted to destroy the Kaʿbah in the year of the Prophet Muhammad's birth. The Meccans' miraculous victory over the Abyssinians and preservation of their Holy Sanctuary led

---

[100] Abū Muḥammad 'Abd al-Malik ibn Hishām ibn Ayyūb al-Ḥimyarī Ibn Hishām, *Al-Sīrah al-Nabawīyah. al-Juz' al-Awwal*, ed. Majdi Fathi Al-Sayyid, 1st ed. (Cairo: Dār al-Sahāba lil-Turāth, 1995), 122.

to an increased religious fervor in the veneration of the Kaʿbah. Mecca would symbolize power and independence among the Arabs, because it did not succumb to the rule of any king, foreign or domestic.[101]

The conflict between Persia and Byzantine made traditional travel and trade routes through Iraq and the Levant dangerous. Therefore, traders traversed Arabia to get back and forth. As such, the southern regions of Yemen and Hadramaut were connected to al-Ḥīrah in the east and to Buṣrā in the north all the way to Gaza and Egypt through Mecca, which was considered a haven. The residents of Mecca generally did not pay taxes. Instead, they taxed pilgrims, traders, and other outsiders, while also hosting them. Its major marketplaces were ʿUkāẓ, al-Majannah, and Dhū al-Majāz, which were major thoroughfares of goods and culture, as poetry matches were characteristic of these gatherings.[102]

Mecca's *Dār al-Nadwah* was like a small congress. Only wealthy men aged forty and over were chosen to join. They made decisions on issues related to business, religion, and finance, since they oversaw scales and weights, interest rates, and the like.[103] The *Dār al-Nadwah* could have also been an enduring Roman-style Mystery School in Arabia. The fact that they had knowledge of computation along with religious matters is telling of their erudition, as the Mysteries were the sites of both worldly

---

[101] Ḍayf, *Al-ʿAṣr al-Jāhilī*, 49.

[102] Ḍayf, *Al-ʿAṣr al-Jāhilī*, 50.

[103] Ḍayf, *Al-ʿAṣr al-Jāhilī*, 51.

and other worldly knowledge. The fact that the *Nadwah* only selected wealthy men over forty is also significant. The Mysteries often considered men over the age of forty to be enlightened and ready for leadership. For example, it is noted that the likes of Pythagoras (ca. 570 to ca. 490 B.C.E.) and Zeno (347-275 B.C.E.), the founder of Stoicism (a Mystery School), only started teaching at the age of forty.[104] Similarly, the Prophet Muhammad, though considered virtuous prior to his prophetic mission, only received revelation at the age of forty. The fact that the Quraysh, particularly the Banū Hāshim, had a type of charisma in relation to other Arab tribes is also significant. Ibn Hishām reports that ʿAmr ibn Munaf, the great grandfather of the Prophet Muhammad, was given the name Hāshim from his cutting up bread for the pilgrims and providing them water.[105] This sacred service was taken very seriously and remained in the line of Hāshim to the time of the Prophet Muhammad and purportedly to this day.

The Muslim historian, al-Masʿūdī, reported that some Sabians regarded the Holy Sanctuary of the Kaʿbah to have once been a Saturnalia shrine, which al-Shahrastānī disputed. Saturnalia shrines were characterized by a black stone accompanied by images of dark-skinned elderly Indian men,

---

[104] Carl Huffman, "Pythagoras," in *The Stanford Encyclopedia of Philosophy*, ed. Edward N. Zalta, Winter 2018 (Stanford: Metaphysics Research Lab, Stanford University, 2018), https://plato.stanford.edu/archives/win2018/entries/pythagoras/, and George Stock, *Stoicism*, Religions Modern and Ancient (London: Archibald Constable & Co., 1908), 3.

[105] Ibn Hishām, *Al-Sīrah al-Nabawīyah. al-Juz' al-Awwal*, 177-9.

one holding an ax, another with a rope, one a carpenter, another a king riding an elephant surrounded by cows and bison.[106] If this was the case, then the Sabians would have considered the Kaʿbah a shrine dedicated to the worship of one of the heavenly bodies. Shawqī Ḍayf states that Sabianism and Chaldean practices came to the Arabs in ancient times because there is evidence of them worshiping the stars and planets. However, he believes that they were more influenced by southern Arabians since they believed in a holy trinity, which consisted of the moon (or *Wadd*), the sun (*Allāt*), and Venus (*'Uzzā*).[107] Yet, Green has also established a relationship between the Arabs and Ḥarranians, whose preeminent deity was the moon god. If we couple this with the understandings of Muslim scholars who recorded the heavenly bodies were worshiped by each tribe in Arabia, we must conclude that the popular religion in Mecca was similar to the Sabianism of Ḥarrān.

Medina

As for Medina, which was known as Yathrib, it was first settled by the *ʿAmāliqah*,[108] another extinct Arab tribe. According to Ḍayf, they

---

[106] Samak, *Al-Ṣābi'ūn*, 69.

[107] Ḍayf, *Al-ʿAṣr al-Jāhilī*, 89.

[108] According to Zaydan, the *ʿAmāliqah* are the ancient Semitic Bedouins who wandered the areas between the Tigris and Euphrates rivers and the Nile. He equates them with the Shāsū or the Hyksos who conquered Egypt. *Al-ʿArab*, 67-9.

remained there until the Jews settled there in the 2nd century C.E. following their expulsion from Palestine by the Romans. They named it *Madīntā*, which is close to the Mandaean word for city or town (for instance, Nazareth is *Niṣrath madinta*). We do not know if they were ethnic Arabs who converted to Judaism, or if they were ethnic Hebrews who adopted the Arabic language, nor do we know their specific sect of Judaism.[109] I assume that they too were the remnants of ancient Sabian groups from the greater Near East. Mandaean literature, for instance, refers to both Jewish and non-Jewish Chaldeans as *Yahuṭaiia* (Yahūd in Arabic). Mandaeans saw them ethnically as one people, but with different religions. Nebuchadnezzar is referred to racially as a *Yahuṭai*, although he was not Jewish.[110] This aligns with al-Andalusī's typology of the *umam*, which labels all peoples from the Arabian Peninsula as Chaldeans.[111]

We can also gather from al-Bīrūnī that he believed the Sabians were a type of Jew, specifically those who were captured in Babylon by Nebuchadnezzar and chose to stay. As such, their religion became a syncretic version of Judaism and Magianism (i.e., Zoroastrianism). He

---

[109] Ḍayf, *Al-ʿAṣr al-Jāhilī*, 53. Some scholars also believe that the Hebrews and Arabs are one people. The Hebrews were distinguished by their monotheism and restrictive religious practices from polytheists. *See* Shahrastānī and Muhammad, *Al-Milal Wa al-Niḥal*, vol. 1, 227-9.

[110] Drower and Buckley, *Mandaeans of Iraq*, 287.

[111] Ṣāʿid al-Andalusī, *Al-Taʿrīf Fī Ṭabaqāt al-Umam* (Beirut: al-Maṭbaʿah al-Kāthalūkīyya li'l Abā' al-Yasūʿīyyīn, 1912), 7.

claims that they eventually populated the Sawād region of Iraq where the current-day Mandaeans dwell. They also believed that they were descendants of Enoch and Seth like the Mandaeans.[112] Given the dearth of information about Christianity and Judaism in the interior of Pre-Islamic Arabia, it is worth investigating the beliefs and origins of Arabian Jews to ascertain whether they generally followed a Ḥanīf doctrine or Sabian doctrine.

Ancient Egyptians

Most premodern Arabic sources consider Sabianism to be the religion of ancient Egypt. The late Nadīm al-Sayyār was able to make a linguistic association between ancient Egyptian religion and Sabianism. He finds that

the ancient Egyptian cognate to *ṣab'a* is pronounced similarly and carries a similar meaning. It is represented (from left to right) by a five-pointed star, a right-facing leg, and left-facing staff, and simply means "star." When coupled with the word, *nīthar*, al-Sayyār believes it to mean angels that reside in the stars. He subsequently demonstrates that it carries the same meaning in Hebrew.[113] Al-Sayyār also discovered in a papyrus scroll the word *ṣabāwi* (knowledge), which is derived from the word *ṣabā* (guidance). He found that the word *ṣabāyat* (teachings, scripture, or

[112] Green, *The City of the Moon God*, 116.

[113] Nadīm al-Sayyār, *Laysū Āliha Wa Lākin Malā'ika* (Cairo, 2020), 142-4.

message) was a derivative of this root as well, leading him to believe that the ancient Egyptians were the Sabians mentioned in the Qur'an. Al-Sayyār was of the belief that the Egyptians received their knowledge from the heavens in the form of revelation and this knowledge was then transmitted by way of tradition.[114] While naming the ancient Egyptian religion as Sabianism can be debated, this evidence demonstrates that the word existed in the ancient Egyptian language and the concept is consistent with how Arabic scholarship has historically depicted Sabianism, as associated with the stars and angels.

Similarly, al-Sayyār sought to debunk the myth that the ancient Egyptians were polytheists. Instead, he argues that they were monotheists who revered the angels. He believes that this confusion lies in the European mistranslation of the word *nīthar* as "god."[115] Al-Sayyār states that early European Egyptologists often looked to Greek and Latin to determine the meanings of ambiguous terminology in the ancient Egyptian language and thus transposed the concept of Greek and Roman deities to Egypt.

However, al-Sayyār, following an Arabic methodology, begins by looking at the word linguistically and terminologically. This approach unravels the word's meaning from its etymology and use in other contexts. Not only that, but he believes as many Arab linguists believe,

---

[114] Nadīm Sayyār, *Qudamā' Al-Misṛīyīn Awwal al-Muwahḥịdīn*, 2nd ed. (Cairo, 1995), 274-6.

[115] This is also commonly transliterated as *neter* or the plural form *neteru*. For this discussion, I am maintaining al-Sayyār's Arabic transliteration.

which is that every letter can reveal an aspect of the word's meaning.[116] In a section with the title "Every letter was originally a word," he determines that the consonantal trilateral root of the word *nīthar* (*n-th-r*) had connotations to "water," "hand," and "mouth" respectively. When joined, *n* means "related to" and *r* means "to speak." The core of the word, however, is the *th* sound in the middle, which is represented by a rope glyph, implying an agreement. He adds that when the vowel *ī* is inserted into the word, it is like the relative adjective suffix in Arabic that shows belonging, which al-Sayyār says literally means "to tie." He then states that in ancient Egypt when two parties wanted to make a contract, they would tie a rope around the two parties and recite the terms of the agreement.[117] Interestingly, when speaking of the Indo-Iranian deity, Mithras, which is spelled in Greek with the letter *θ* for the *th* sound, Bremmer states that its original meaning is unknown, "but there is some consensus that it must originally have meant something like 'contract'."[118] Al-Sayyār's point in this elaborate treatment of the word,

---

[116] Nadīm al-Sayyār, *Laysū Āliha Wa Lākin Malā'ika* (Cairo, 2020), 60.

[117] Sayyār, *Laysū*, 62-8. In addition, al-Sayyar notes that this is a practice among the Chagga people who live along the northern borders of Tanzania. He states that this practice that was either brought to them by the ancient Egyptians or their ancestors were themselves ancient Egyptians. Al-Sayyar evidences both opinions in the writings of Herodotus. A quarter million Egyptians migrated to Ethiopia and built a civilization there and some are known to have migrated as far as the Niger River. George G.M. James believes that the inheritors of the Ancient Mystery Schools fled deeper into Africa and spread their teachings there.

[118] Bremmer, *Initiation*, 126.

nīthar, is to say that if understood properly, it does not mean god, rather, it means something that represents the divine, like an angel.

Undoubtedly, the centrality of astrological "deities" is a major point of convergence between Egyptian and pre-Islamic Arabian religion, the Greek Mysteries, and Mandaean and Ḥarrānian Sabianism. As we know, planet names in English all refer to Roman deities. However, according to al-Shahrastānī's analysis of Sabianism, these so-called deities represent angels (or *jinn*), who serve as intercessors between humans and God.[119] In this framework, the stars are the embodiment of the angels in the sky while idols are the embodiment of angels on earth. People pray and sacrifice to these astral and terrestrial embodiments of angels with the belief that God is too exalted and transcendent to accept worship from human beings directly. Consequently, humans must offer worship through God's elected beings in the heavens and the earth in order to purify and validate their worship. It is for this reason that Muslim scholars referred to Sabians sometimes as angel worshipers and other times as idol worshipers.

---

[119] Al-Shahrastānī explains that there were those among the Arabs who followed the religion of the Sabians and astrologers, by following the stars in all their dealings. They believed that they were worshiping angels, who were considered the daughters of God, but al-Shahrastānī believes they were worshiping *jinn* in actuality. *Al-Milal Wa al-Niḥal*, vol. 3, 660.

Egyptian Religion

Maimonides, the 12th century Jewish polymath from Cordoba, believed that the basis of Jewish law and rituals was in response to Egyptian Sabian beliefs and practices. His *Guide for the Perplexed* suggests that Jewish law is an inversion of the practices of the ancient Egyptian Sabians. He believed that the Judaic laws decreed by Moses were instituted to undermine the beliefs and practices of the Sabians to which the Children of Israel became accustom. Furthermore, Maimonides claims that the remnants of the Sabian religion persisted in the extreme north among the Turks and the extreme south among the Indians, as well as all those living according to pagan customs. This further corroborates George G.M. James' notion that the Mystery Schools survived in the interior of African and most indigenous populations who are characterized as pagans.[120]

Similarly, the 12th century Egyptian scholar, Muhammad al-Idrīsī, refers to Egypt's ancient religion as Sabianism without qualifying his usage of the term. This shows that it was common to do such in his time. In his book about the two pyramids of Giza,[121] *Anwār 'Ulwīyy al-Ajrām fī al-Kashf 'an Asrār al-Ahrām (Light on the Voluminous Bodies to Reveal the Secrets of the Pyramids)*, he narrates numerous folk tales about ancient

---

[120] Jonathan Elukin, "Maimonides and the Rise and Fall of the Sabians: Explaining Mosaic Laws and the Limits of Scholarship," *Journal of the History of Ideas* 63, no. 4 (2002): 620-1.

[121] In al-Idrīsī's time only two of the Great Pyramids of Giza were visible.

Egypt. For instance, he relates that Enoch (who he also equates with the Islamic prophet, Idrīs and Hermes) lived before the Great Deluge and he wrote numerous books of metered poetry in the ancient Egyptian language on a variety of high and lower order sciences in the style of the philosophers. He learned of an upcoming cataclysm through his knowledge of the stars, but he did not know if it would be in the form of fire, water, or the sword. So, they created *barbā* (pl. *barābī*) as a protection and way of preserving their history. *Barābī* refers to the statues, monuments, and other structures known in ancient Egypt that were made of stone and clay. They figured that if the cataclysm were a flood, the clay would be wiped away, but the stone would remain. If it were fire, then the clay would remain, if it were the sword then everything would remain.[122] In another passage, al-Idrīsī cites the son of the acclaimed 10th century Egyptian historian, Abū ʿUmar al-Kindī, who witnessed Sabians from Ḥarrān making pilgrimage to the pyramids at Giza because they believed them to be the graves of Hermes and Agathodaemon.[123]

In Mandaean mythology, there is also a great deal of overlap with ancient Egypt. They believe that an angel by the name of Pthāhīl, analogous to the Egyptian deity Ptah, created the first race of humans. He created earth and the body of man in his image with the help of the "Mother of

---

[122] Muḥammad ibn ʻAbd al-ʻAzīz al-Idrīsī and Ulrich Haarmann, *Anwār ʻUlwīyy Al-Ajrām Fī al-Kashf ʻan Asrār al-Ahrām*, Nusūṣ wa-Dirāsāt 38 (Bayrūt: Frānts Shtāyrir, 1991), 93-4.

[123] Idrīsī and Haarmann, *Anwār*, 22.

Darkness," Rūhā, and the seven planets. This in turn prepared the souls of human beings to descend from the "Realm of Light" and occupy human bodies. After 216,000 years, Rūhā returned and attempted to destroy the human race in a natural disaster. In the following epoch, which lasted for 156,000 years, the Nāṣoraeans appeared, but they would be afflicted with a cataclysmic fire. The third age would last 100,000 years before it was destroyed by a great flood. This was the flood that Noah and his son, Shem, survived, becoming the Nāṣoraean authority in his time. In their narrative, Danānūkht, also identified as Enoch, Hermes, and Idrīs, lived after the Great Deluge. He would emerge as a leader of the Nāṣoraeans, who built the pyramids, and taught the arts of civilization and wisdom teachings to mankind. They claim that his son, *Sāb* (spelled with the Arabic letter *sīn*), was buried in one of the pyramids and the Sabian religion, the religion of ancient Egypt, takes its name from him and they practice the same religion as the Mandaeans.[124]

In Western scholarship, the religion of ancient Egypt is called the Mystery Schools by the likes of George G.M. James, Cedric Robinson, and Martin Bernal, which they also claim is the parent religion of Greek religion and philosophy, and, to an extent, the religious thought of the greater Near East. They depict Egypt as an intellectual and religious destination for pilgrims from all over the ancient world, like Egypt's position in classical Islamic times and even today.[125] Moreover, they emphasize the fact that

---

[124] Mājidī, *Al-Mandā'īyah*, 37-9.

[125] James, *Stolen Legacy,* 30.

it was an advanced Black African civilization. According to Robinson, the Egyptian Mysteries, with its intellectual and scientific knowledge, is what rescued the crumbling Greek civilization around 600 B.C.E.[126] Both James and Bernal's thesis is that post-Enlightenment Europe unduly attributed the accomplishments of the ancient Egyptians to the Greeks, a fact that has been hidden from public knowledge in modern times.

Bernal claims that the destruction of the Serapis temple and its library in Alexandria in 390 C.E. followed by the murder of Hypatia, a philosopher and mathematician, marked the end of the Egyptian Mysteries and ushered in the Christian Dark Ages. In his attempt to unravel exactly what led to the decline of the Mysteries and the salience of Christianity, he suggests that Egyptians had a strong belief that major events in their society were governed by the stars. Between 50 B.C.E. and 150 C.E., the astrological calendar marked the shift from the age of Aries to the age of Pisces, and the dawning of a new era. He takes this as the death of the ancient Egyptian religion and its rebirth as Christianity. Under the new

---

[126] Cedric J. Robinson, *Black Marxism: The Making of the Black Radical Tradition* (Chapel Hill, N.C: University of North Carolina Press, 2000), 83-4, *cf* Guenon believes this to be the start of the Kali Yuga, the Dark Ages according to Indian cosmology, Rene Guenon, *Spiritual Authority and Temporal Power*, trans. Henry D. Fohr and Samuel D. Fohr (New York: Sophia Perennis, 1929), 11.

banner, it would maintain the Mysteries-influenced intellectual currents of Hermeticism, Neo-Platonism, and Gnosticism.[127]

Majūs

Magianism was once called *Jawidan Khard* or the Eternal Wisdom. Kapadia traces it to the Persian king, Hoshung, who imparted its teachings. However, during a period of duress the people turned to idol worship and thus polytheism spread throughout the Aryan lands.[128] A ruler named Jamshid instituted a number of reforms including the establishment of the solar calendar and a caste system that divided people into four groups: 1) religious scholars, 2) administrators of the divine law, 3) soldiers, and 4) a working class of merchants, artisans, agriculturalists, and so on. He then wanted the people to worship him. Although they were idolaters, they were pleased with worshiping images of the past not living beings. This led to turmoil in Persia until a Syrian ruler conquered it.[129]

Though there are discrepancies concerning the exact era he was born, Zoroaster was the righteous child of righteous and noble descent who was

---

[127] Martin Bernal and G. A. Gaballa, *Black Athena: The Afroasiatic Roots of Classical Civilization*, vol. 1, 3 vols. (New Brunswick, NJ: Rutgers University Press, 1987), 121-34.

[128] S.A. Kapadia, *The Teachings of Zoroaster and the Philosophy of the Parsi Religion*, 2nd ed., The Wisdom of the East Series (London: John Murray, 1913), 14–15.

[129] Kapadia, 15–17.

destined to preach monotheism to idolatrous Aryan people. Legend states that he was born in Ray to pious monotheistic parents. His father, Pourushaspa and mother, Dogdho, prayed for virtuous progeny, so they consulted the ninth chapter of their holy book and prayed to be blessed with such a child. Zoroaster's mother saw a vision of him in a dream after he was conceived in which he was approaching heaven to acquire the Zend-Avesta scripture and "sacred fire" from God. It is also reported that he laughed the moment of his birth, and that people were attracted to his aura before he even reached manhood.[130]

The teachings of Zoroaster cannot be described as anything but Ḥanīf. He strove to turn people away from their idols and to the worship of the *Ahura Mazda* (the All-Knowing Deity). In his theology, God created the universe in six stages: 1) the heavens, 2) water, 3) earth, 4) plants, 5) animals, and 6) mankind, who was made to act according to his heart and his mind. He did not teach dualism, but merely the existence of good and evil deeds. Good deeds, he taught, were to serve the poor and indigent, cultivate the soil, and live a life of temperance and chastity. Likewise, he taught that six archangels protected and governed over aspects of creation.[131]

According to al-Bīrūnī, Magianism is the original religion of Persia, but it was later integrated into Zoroastrianism. Some were monotheists

---

[130] Kapadia, 17–18.

[131] Kapadia, 18–41.

(referred to historically as Mazdeans) and they were supported by the monarch. Others were polytheists dedicated to the *Shamsīya*, the sun-worshiping sect (referred to historically as Daevaeans) and they were mostly driven into India, but the Muslims eventually displaced their lasting remnants in Persia. Although the polytheists practiced some ancient customs, al-Bīrūnī claims that those customs were derived from the ancient people of Ḥarrān. He then emphasizes the position that the true Sabians were the Jews of Babylon who embraced aspects of the Babylonian Magian religion. This made their religion a syncretic mix of Judaism and Magianism. Al-Bīrūnī compared them to the Samaritans who also moved from Babylon to Syria.[132] His perspective does not equate Magianism with Sabianism. Rather, he sees the mixture of polytheistic Magianism with a monotheistic religion like Zoroastrianism or Judaism as Sabianism.

An inquiry into Mithraism provides us with a deeper look into Magianism and how Persian Zoroastrianism drifted into Sabianism. The cult of Mithras was the dominant type of Magianism and was known in its Persian and Roman forms. According to Payam Nabarz, Mithras or *mehr* means "love," "sun," and "friend." He is known as the sun god and friend or protector of the warrior. Mandrake is referred to as *mehr giah*, a plant used for love potions. Mithras was worshiped as early as the 2nd century B.C.E. Mithras as known as *Mitra* in the Indian Vedas and was considered the "lord of heavenly light," "protector of truth," and was invoked when

---

132 Bīrūnī and Sachau, *Chronology*, 314.

making oaths.[133] Nabarz asserts that Mithras was demoted to the rank of an angel in Zoroastrianism and is named among the *yazatas* (protective spirits), who is analogous to the Egyptian god, Ma'at. According to Nabarz, Zoroastrianism incorporated aspects of Mithraism. He says that their priests continue to carry the mace that symbolizes Mithras. He also states that the temple in which they keep their fire is called *dare-e mehr* (the court of Mithras). Some have even elevated Mithras to an intercessor with *Ahura Mazda*.[134]

It is important to note that the Persians believed that Hermes was from Mesopotamia, not Egypt, meaning that the source of material and metaphysical knowledge originated with their civilization. While the figure of Hermes is a common denominator among all the Sabian and Ḥanīf factions, the Denkard, one of the primary texts on Zoroastrianism, regards all knowledge, religious and secular, as being derived from the Avesta (i.e., the canon of Zoroastrian scripture). It was also a pervading view among the Persians that Zoroaster wrote the books of knowledge in all the languages of the world.[135] Aramaic speakers living in Mesopotamia have long since attached themselves to the Babylonian – Persian legacy, which only strengthened following the persecution of non-Chalcedonian

---

[133] See Bremmer, *Initiation*, 126 and Sayyār, *Laysū*, 68.

[134] Payam Nabarz, *Mysteries of Mithras: The Pagan Belief That Shaped the Christian World* (Vermont: Inner Traditions International, Limited, 2005), 7–10.

[135] Dimitri Gutas, *Greek Thought, Arabic Culture: The Graeco-Arabic Translation Movement in Baghdad and Early 'Abbāsid Society (2nd-4th/8th-10th Centuries)* (New York: Routledge, 1998), 41–42.

Aramaic speaking Christians at the hands of the Roman Byzantines. The Abbasids also embraced this sentiment; they saw themselves as continuing the reestablishment of Persian knowledge.[136]

[136] Gutas, 43.

Chapter Four
Revealing the Mystery

> “
>
> أَمْ تَقُولُونَ إِنَّ إِبْرَٰهِـۧمَ وَإِسْمَـٰعِيلَ وَإِسْحَـٰقَ وَيَعْقُوبَ وَٱلْأَسْبَاطَ كَانُوا
> هُودًا أَوْ نَصَـٰرَىٰ ۗ قُلْ ءَأَنتُمْ أَعْلَمُ أَمِ ٱللَّهُ ۗ وَمَنْ أَظْلَمُ مِمَّن كَتَمَ شَهَـٰدَةً
> عِندَهُۥ مِنَ ٱللَّهِ ۗ وَمَا ٱللَّهُ بِغَـٰفِلٍ عَمَّا تَعْمَلُونَ
>
> *Or do you all say that Abraham, Ishmael, Isaac, Jacob, and the Progeny were Hūd and Naṣārā? Say: Are you all more knowledgeable of God? And who is more unjust than the one who conceals a testimony he has from God. God is not heedless of what you do.*
> *(al-Baqarah: 140)*

Our brief exploration into the history of the Mystery Schools under Christendom and Islam and its various expressions has taken us through the annals of history, Greek, Persian, Egyptian, Arabic, Syriac, and Mandaic languages. We also took a cursory look into esoteric and African-centered sources on the Mysteries. Yet, this exploration is not just an exercise in information gathering but it is an opportunity for us to reflect upon our fundamental understanding of religious history and the spiritual debates of our current times. For followers of Abrahamic religions, an understanding of the Mystery Schools and Sabianism can lead to a deeper understanding of scripture and divine law. This perspective fills some major gaps that have even eluded past and present experts of the topic.

Knowledge of the Mystery Schools and Sabians has the potential to establish a new framework for understanding religious history, the roots of religious conflicts in the West, and classifying current religious trends. Much of our current understanding of religious history is shaped by our personal biases, whether they are shaped by incontrovertible religiosity or overly skeptical secularism. However, the sources of history are telling us a different story. They are saying that a division of beliefs has existed throughout religious history. One doctrine values the concept of one immutable deity who cares for the creation, the subordination of the angelic realm, and salvation through grace. The teachers of this doctrine were human prophets who received revelation and authority from God to teach this message. The other doctrine also maintained a belief in one immutable deity, but took the position that God is unconcerned with human affairs and angelic beings play a more active role in the lives of mankind. Therefore, the angels are more worthy of worship. Moreover, they reasoned that it was possible for God and His attributes to exist within creation, and they could manifest in various elements, images, and people. Additionally, they argued that salvation is not attained by worship or obedience to God and His prophets, but through self-knowledge, strict ascetism, and finding the divinity within themselves. Therefore, a prophet or saved individual is one who has advanced to the state of an angel or god.

Of course, the Muslim view sets forth clear distinctions between God, angel, man, and *jinn*. God is unified and transcendent, but also concerned with the affairs of people. He is the uncreated Creator of the universe and everything in existence. Angels are beings made of light, as many Sabians also believe, but they only do as God commands them to. They do not exhibit free will or the tendency to deviate from the will of God as imagined in much Sabian mythology. And so, it is easier to discern angelic influence and that of the *jinn*. The *jinn*, as beings made of fire, are led by the avowed enemy of mankind, Satan or the Shayṭān. Therefore, any accusations of corruption and evil can only be attributed to the *jinn*.

This understanding revives a way of looking at religious scripture and conflicts throughout history. As I demonstrated with the story of Abraham, the Sabian backstory can add another dimension to the interpretation of scripture. Perhaps a similar methodology can be applied to instances in the Qur'an that mention God's command to the angels to bow before Adam. Since Sabians believe that the angels are worthy of worship, it is unimaginable for them to bow before a man.

As for religious conflict, we have looked at the debate between al-Ghazālī and Ibn Rushd. As the greatest scholar of Aristotelian thought, whose philosophical school is a proponent of the eternity of the universe, Ibn Rushd represented Sabianism among the Muslims, whereas al-Ghazālī represented the Ḥanīfs. Perhaps, retracing these arguments and sentiments to the early divisions in Islam between *Mutakallimūn* (Speculative Theologians) and *Muḥadithūn* (Traditionalists) over the createdness of the Qur'an, the role of human rational thought, and religious authority. Even experts like Nimrod Hurvitz have noticed the connection of such debates to the Sabians: "It is worth noting that this type of controversy [i.e., the *Miḥnah*] emerged in all three monotheistic faiths, Judaism, Christianity, and Islam, particularly when they came across Greek science and logic."[137]

Finally, understanding the positions of the Mysteries or Sabians provides us a framework for addressing current religious trends in the West. Although we have lost the terms of these ancient movements, the beliefs and arguments still exist. The Theosophical Society was one of the first movements to promote Sabian-style beliefs in the West. The group's leader, Helena Blavatsky, was vehemently anti-Ḥanīf. She believed that Christians were arrogant hypocrites who used religion to gain wealth and power through deceptive means. Meanwhile, her biographer uncovered many contradictions and untruths in her own life, exposing her as the hypocrite and deceiver.[138]

Nevertheless, the Theosophical Society would serve as the springboard to American Sabianism. Several occult, New Age, and "spiritual" movements would emerge throughout the 20th century reiterating the positions of the Sabians. They deride religion – primarily Ḥanīf religions – as systems of social control and the source of division and prejudice in the world, but the sharpest divisions in religious history have been initiated by Sabian factions, who polluted the original sacred doctrines

---

137 Nimrod Hurvitz, "Al-Ma'mūn (r. 198/813–218/833) and the Miḥna," in *The Oxford Handbook of Islamic Theology*, ed. Sabine Schmidtke, Oxford Handbooks (Oxford, United Kingdom: Oxford University Press, 2016), 658.

138 Gary Lachman, *Madame Blavatsky : The Mother of Modern Spirituality* (New York: Jeremy P. Tarcher/Penguin Books, 2012), 323–24.

and rituals. Their myths, disputations, and philosophizing are what led to religious confusion and dissension.

In the 21st century, young and older people alike eschew religion based on Blavatsky's rhetoric and that of other Sabian-style movements, but few have sought to investigate the reality of the matter. We have in *Islam and the Ancient Mysteries* a new – rather, resurrected – approach to studying religious history and classifying religious doctrine. It is akin to Renè Guenon's Traditionalism, which recognizes an intrinsic esoteric doctrine present in all religions, while also acknowledging certain criteria to judge a religion's authenticity. As we learn more about Sabians, Mystery Schools, Gnostics, and the history of late Antiquity and early Islam, we will find this a more viable mode of looking at religious history.

BIBLIOGRAPHY

Averroës. *The Attitude of Islam Towards Science and Philosophy: A Translation of Ibn Rushd's (Averroës) Famous Treatise Faslul-al-Maqal*. Translated by Aadil Amin Kak. Sarup & Sons, 2003.

Andalusī, Ṣāʿid al-. *Al-Taʿrīf Fī Ṭabaqāt al-Umam*. Beirut: al-Maṭbaʿah al-Kāthalūkīyya li'l Abā' al-Yasūʿīyyīn, 1912.

Ando, Clifford. "Religious Affiliation and Political Belonging from Cicero to Theodosius." *Acta Classica* 64, no. 1 (2021): 9–28. https://doi.org/10.1353/acl.2021.0013.

Berkey, Jonathan Porter. *The Formation of Islam: Religion and Society in the Near East, 600-1800*. Themes in Islamic History 2. New York: Cambridge University Press, 2003.

Bernal, Martin, and G. A. Gaballa. *Black Athena: The Afroasiatic Roots of Classical Civilization*. Vol. 1. 3 vols. New Brunswick, NJ: Rutgers University Press, 1987.

Bīrūnī, Muḥammad ibn Aḥmad, and Eduard Sachau. *The Chronology of Ancient Nations: An English Version of the Arabic Text of the Athâr-Ul-Bâkiya of Albîrûnî, or, "Vestiges of the Past."* London: Oriental Translation Fund of Great Britain and Ireland, 1879.

Blois, François de. "Naṣrānī (Ναζωραῖος) and Ḥanīf (Ἐθνικός): Studies on the Religious Vocabulary of Christianity and of Islam." *Bulletin of the School of Oriental and African Studies, University of London* 65, no. 1 (2002): 1–30.

Bremmer, Jan N. *Initiation into the Mysteries of the Ancient World*. Münchner Vorlesungen Zu Antiken Welten 1. Boston: De Gruyter, 2014.

Buck, Christopher. "The Identity of the Sabi'un: An Historical Quest." *The Muslim World* 74, no. 3–4 (1984): 172–86.

Buckley, Jorunn Jacobsen. *The Mandaeans: Ancient Texts and Modern People*. American Academy of Religion the Religions Series. New York: Oxford University Press, 2002.

Burkert, Walter. *Ancient Mystery Cults*. Cambridge: Harvard University Press, 1987.

Crone, Patricia, and Michael Cook. *Hagarism: The Making of the Islamic World*. Cambridge: Cambridge University Press, 1977.

Ḍayf, Shawqi. *Al-ʿAṣr al-Jāhilī*. 11th ed. Vol. 1. Tarikh Al-Adab al-'Arabi. Cairo: Dār al-Ma'ārif, 1960.

Drower, E. S. (Ethel Stefana), and Jorunn Jacobsen Buckley. *The Mandaeans of Iraq and Iran Their Cults, Customs, Magic Legends, and Folklore*. London: Oxford University Press, 1937.

Dunstan, William E. *Ancient Rome*. Blue Ridge Summit: Rowman & Littlefield Publishers, 2002.

Elukin, Jonathan. "Maimonides and the Rise and Fall of the Sabians: Explaining Mosaic Laws and the Limits of Scholarship." *Journal of the History of Ideas* 63, no. 4 (2002): 619–37. https://doi.org/10.2307/3654163.

Errington, R. M. *Roman Imperial Policy from Julian to Theodosius*. Studies in the History of Greece and Rome. Chapel Hill: University of North Carolina Press, 2006.

Ghazālī, Abu Hamid. *Al-Ghazali's Tahāfut al-Falāsifah: Incoherence of the Philosophers*. Translated by Sabih Ahmad Kamali. Pakistan Philosophical Congress Publication, no. 3. Lahore: Pakistan Philosophical Congress, 1963.

Grant, Robert M. *Gnosticism and Early Christianity*. Lectures on the History of Religions. New York: Columbia University Press, 1959.

Green, Tamara M. *The City of the Moon God: Religious Traditions of Harran*. Religions in the Graeco-Roman World, 0927-7633, v. 114. Leiden: E.J. Brill, 1992.

Guenon, Rene. *Perspectives on Initiation*. Edited by Samuel D. Fohr. Translated by Henry D. Fohr. New York: Sophia Perennis, 1946.

———. *Spiritual Authority and Temporal Power*. Translated by Henry D. Fohr and Samuel D. Fohr. New York: Sophia Perennis, 1929.

———. *The Crisis of the Modern World*. Translated by Marco Pallis, Arthur Osborne, and Richard C. Nicholson. New York: Sophia Perennis, 1946.

———. *The Reign of Quantity and the Signs of the Times*. Translated by Lord Northbourne. New York: Sophia Perennis, 1945.

Gutas, Dimitri. *Greek Thought, Arabic Culture: The Graeco-Arabic Translation Movement in Baghdad and Early 'Abbāsid Society (2nd-4th/8th-10th Centuries)*. New York: Routledge, 1998.

Hillar, Marian. *From Logos to Trinity: The Evolution of Religious Beliefs from Pythagoras to Tertullian*. Cambridge: Cambridge University Press, 2012.

Hines, Maurice. "Interpretatio Islamica and the Unraveling of the Ancient Sabian Mysteries." American University in Cairo, 2023. https://fount.aucegypt.edu/etds/2052.

Huffman, Carl. "Pythagoras." In *The Stanford Encyclopedia of Philosophy*, edited by Edward N. Zalta, Winter 2018. Stanford: Metaphysics Research Lab, Stanford University, 2018. https://plato.stanford.edu/archives/win2018/entries/pythagoras/.

Ibn al-Nadīm, Abū al-Faraj Muḥammad ibn Isḥaq. *The Fihrist of Al-Nadim: A Tenth Century Survey of Muslim Culture*. Translated by Bayard Dodge. Vol. 2. New York: Columbia University Press, 1970.

Ibn Hishām, Abū Muḥammad 'Abd al-Malik ibn Hishām ibn Ayyūb al-Ḥimyarī. *Al-Sīra al-Nabawīyah. al-Juz' al-Awwal*. Edited by Majdi Fathi Al-Sayyid. 1st ed. Cairo: Dār al-Saḥāba lil-Turāth, 1995.

Ibn Manẓūr, Muhammad ibn Mukarram ibn ʿAlī. *Lisān al-ʿArab*. Vol. 5. Beirut: Dār Ṣādir, 1300.

Ibn Nadīm, Abū al-Faraj Muḥammad ibn Isḥaq. *Al-Fihrist*. Beirut: Dar al-Ma'rifah, 937.

Idrīsī, Muḥammad ibn 'Abd al-'Azīz al-, and Ulrich Haarmann. *Anwār 'Ulwīyy Al-Ajrām Fī al-Kashf 'an Asrār al-Ahrām*. Nuṣūṣ wa-Dirāsāt 38. Bayrūt: Frānts Shtāyrir, 1991.

James, George G.M. *Stolen Legacy: Greek Philosophy Is Stolen Egyptian Philosophy*. New York: Philosophical Library, 1954.

Johnston, Sarah Iles, ed. *Ancient Religions*. Cambridge: Belknap Press of Harvard University Press, 2007.

Kapadia, S.A. *The Teachings of Zoroaster and the Philosophy of the Parsi Religion*. 2nd ed. The Wisdom of the East Series. London: John Murray, 1913.

Keys, David. *Catastrophe: An Investigation into the Origins of the Modern World*. New York: Ballantine Books, 1999.

Lachman, Gary. *Madame Blavatsky : The Mother of Modern Spirituality*. New York: Jeremy P. Tarcher/Penguin Books, 2012.

Laistner, M.L.W. *Christianity and Pagan Culture in the Later Roman Empire*. Ithaca, NY: Cornell University Press, 1951.

Mackey, Albert G. *An Encyclopedia of Freemasonry and Its Kindred Sciences: Comprising the Whole Range of Arts, Sciences and Literature as Connected with the Institution.* 2 vols. New York: Masonic History Company, 1914.

Mājidī, Khazʿal al-. *Al-Mithūlūjīyah al-Mandāʾīyah.* Damascus: Dār al-Nīnawā, 2010.

Meyer, Marvin W., ed. *The Ancient Mysteries: A Sourcebook of Sacred Texts.* 1st ed. Philadelphia: University of Pennsylvania Press, 1999.

Morrow, John A. *The Covenants of the Prophet Muhammad with the Christians of the World.* Kettering, Ohio: Angelico Press, Sophia Perennis, 2013.

Nabarz, Payam. *Mysteries of Mithras: The Pagan Belief That Shaped the Christian World.* Vermont: Inner Traditions International, Limited, 2005.

Origen. *On First Principles.* Translated by John Behr. 2 vols. Oxford: Oxford University Press, 2017.

Osman, Ghada. "Pre-Islamic Arab Converts to Christianity in Mecca and Medina: An Investigation into the Arabic Sources." *The Muslim World* 95, no. 1 (2005): 67–80. https://doi.org/10.1111/j.1478-1913.2005.00079.x.

Pike, Albert. *Morals and Dogma of the Ancient and Accepted Scottish Rite of Freemasonry.* Charleston, SC: Supreme Council of the Thirty Third Degree for the Southern Jurisdiction of the United States, 1871.

Pingree, David. "The Sābians of Harrān and the Classical Tradition." *International Journal of the Classical Tradition* 9, no. 1 (June 1, 2002): 8–35. https://doi.org/10.1007/BF02901729.

Qurṭubī, Abū ʿAbd Allah Muḥammad ibn ʾAẖmad al-ʾAnṣārī. *Al-Jāmiʿ Li ʾAḥkām al-Qurʾān*. Vol. 1. 21 vols. Riyad: Dar Alam al-Kutub, 2003.

Rabīʿī, Fāḍil al-. *Al-Masīḥ al-ʿArabī: Al-Naṣrānīyyah Fī al-Jazīrah al-ʿArabīyyah Wa al-Ṣirāʾ al-Bīzanṭī al-Fārisī*. Beirut: Riad El-Rayyes Books, 2009.

Robinson, Cedric J. *Black Marxism: The Making of the Black Radical Tradition*. Chapel Hill, N.C: University of North Carolina Press, 2000.

Samak, ʿAbdullah ʿAlī. *Al-Ṣābiʾūn*. 1st ed. Cairo: Maktabat al-Ādāb, 1995.

Sayyār, Nadīm. *Qudamāʾ Al-Misṛīyīn Awwal al-Muwahḥịdīn*. 2nd ed. Cairo, 1995.

Sayyār, Nadīm al-. *Laysū Āliha Wa Lākin Malāʾika*. Cairo, 2020.

Schmidtke, Sabine, ed. *The Oxford Handbook of Islamic Theology*. Oxford Handbooks. Oxford, United Kingdom: Oxford University Press, 2016. http://swbplus.bsz-bw.de/bsz445705639inh.htm.

Shahrastānī, Muhammad ibn ʿAbd al-Karīm al-, and Ahmad Fahmi Muhammad. *Al-Milal Wa al-Niḥal*. 2nd ed. 3 vols. Beirut: Dār al-Kutub al-ʿIlmīyyah, 1992.

Stock, George. *Stoicism*. Religions Modern and Ancient. London: Archibald Constable & Co., 1908.

Stroumsa, Sarah. *Maimonides in His World: Portrait of a Mediterranean Thinker*. Jews, Christians, and Muslims from the Ancient to the Modern World. Princeton, N.J: Princeton University Press, 2009.

Van Bladel, Kevin Thomas. *From Sasanian Mandaeans to Ṣābians of the Marshes*. Leiden Studies in Islam and Society, volume 6. Boston: Brill, 2017.

Wansbrough, John E. *Quranic Studies: Sources and Methods of Scriptural Interpretation*. London Oriental Series, v. 31. Oxford: Oxford University Press, 1977.

Zaydan, Jurji. *Al-ʻArab Qabl al-Islām*. 3rd ed. Cairo: Dar al-Hilal, 1922.

ʻAlī, Jawwād. *Al-Mufaṣṣal Fī Tārīkh al-ʻArab Qabl al-Islām*. 3rd ed. 10 vols. Baghdad: University of Baghdad, 1947.

Index

A

Abraham (prophet), 18-24, 70, 72, 81
Abū Sahl ibn Nawbakht, 54
Adam, 72, 74
Afrocentrism, 9, 13, 44, 94
Alexander the Great, 54
Angelology, 38, 42, 102
angels, 22, 25, 74, 87-93
Arabia, 19, 25, 63, 71, 76, 80-87
Aramaic, 18, 50, 66, 75, 99
Ardashīr (Persian King), 55
Arians (Christian group), 15
Aryans, 96
astral worship, 21, 90
astrology, 36, 95

B

Babylon, 12, 20, 25, 55, 71, 86, 98, 99
Barābī, 92
Bīrūnī, Abū Rayḥān Muhammad, 72, 86
Blavatsky, Helena, 104
Buddhism, 15

C

Carrhae. *See* Ḥarrān
Chaldeans, 22, 86
Chosroes I (Persian King), 56-57, 67
Chosroes II (Persian King), 56, 57
circumcision, 77
Clement, 36
Constantine, 43, 45
Council of Nicaea, 43, 46

D-F

Dār al-Nadwah, 83
Edessa, 67
Egypt, 25, 33, 36, 44, 47-55, 63, 64, 71, 83, 85, 87-95
ellipsis, 23
Enoch. *See* Idrīs
epoptes, 29, 30
esoterism, 14, 32
Freemasons, 14, 32, 44

G

Ghassanids, 79
Ghazalī, Abū Ḥamid, 60, 103
Gnostics, 16, 17, 26, 37, 38, 41, 49, 57, 64, 70, 75, 95, 105
Greece, 16, 29, 30, 31, 51, 69, 80, 88-90, 94
Guenon, Renè, 32, 35, 44, 48, 78, 94, 105, 109

H

Ḥanbal, Aḥmad ibn. *See* Inquisition (Miḥnah)
Ḥanīf, 18-19, 24, 25, 77, 78, 81
ḥanpa, 18, 69
Ḥarrān, 25, 57, 64-72, 76, 93, 98
Heraclius (Roman Emperor), 56, 57
Hermes, 36, 68, 69, 92, 93
hierophant, 29
Hinduism, 15

I

Ibn Rushd, 60, 103
idol worship, 25
Idrīs (prophet), 92-93
Inquisition (Miḥnah), 65, 103
interpretatio, 12, 34, 68, 78

J-K

James, George G. M., 9-10, 13, 28, 36, 44, 63, 64, 91, 94
Jesus (prophet), 47, 74-77
Jews, 15, 72, 76, 77, 85, 91, 98
jinn, 42, 90, 102-103
Julian (Roman Emperor), 46, 49
Justinian (Roman Emperor), 48, 57, 63, 66, 79, 80
Kaʿbah, 80, 82, 84
Khawad (Persian King), 67

M

Ma'mūn (Abbasid Caliph), 69, 73
Ma'mūn (Caliph), 59, 65
Magians, 14, 17, 57, 63, 86, 96, 97, 98
Maimonides, 66, 91
Mandaeans, 15, 17, 63, 70-76, 86, 94
Manichaeans, 15, 75
Maurice (Roman Emperor), 56-57, 66
Mazdaeans, 15
Mithras, 49, 68, 98-99, 111
Moors, 9, 10, 63
Moses (prophet), 19, 91
Muḥadithūn, 103
Mutakallimūn, 103
mystai. *See* Mystery Schools
mystêrion. *See* Mystery Schools
Mystery Schools, 17, 24, 30-34, 42, 46, 48, 64, 66, 68, 71, 76, 79, 82, 89, 91, 94
  Bacchic Mysteries, 33, 50
  Dionysiac Mysteries, 33
  Egyptian Mysteries, 36, 94, 95
  Eleusinian Mysteries, 31, 33
  Greater Mysteries, 30, 34, 35, 74
  Korybantes Mysteries, 31
  Lesser Mysteries, 34
  Mithraic Mysteries, 33
  Orphic Mysteries, 33, 50
  Stoicism, 35, 83, 84
mystes, 29, 30

N-O

Naṣārā, 76-79
Nāṣoraeans, 22, 63, 73-79, 87, 93
Nebuchadnezzar, 86
Neo-Plantonism, 17, 57, 95
Noah (prophet), 19, 93
Nock, Arthur Darby, 47-49
Nuʿmān II (King of Ḥīrā), 67
oaths, 29, 30
Origen, 60

P

pantheism, 26
Philo (philosopher), 47
polytheism, 11, 18, 19, 38, 57, 96
Pontifex Maximus, 46, 48
Ptah, 93
Pythagoras, 83, 84

R

reincarnation, 26
Rome, 42-48, 50, 63, 72, 79, 80, 82, 85, 88, 90
Rūhā, 93

S

Sabians, 11-25, 28, 35, 37, 38, 41, 42, 55, 57, 63-70, 76, 77, 84-93, 98, 102-105, 108
Sabūr (Persian King), 55
Salvation, 38
Samaritans, 15, 98
Saturnalia, 84
Seth, 87
Slavs, 52
syncretism, 12, 17, 34, 59, 78, 86, 98
Syriac, 69, 73, 75

T-Z

Theodosius I, 42, 46
Theosophy, 11, 44, 64, 104, 105
Traditionalism. *See* Guenon, Renè
ummah, 20
Universe, eternal, 8, 37, 60, 102
Yahuṭaiia. *See* Jews
Yūrbā, 20
Zeno, 83
Zoroastrianism, 25, 64, 86, 97, 98

Made in the USA
Monee, IL
12 June 2025

c30b47e2-94f6-4557-863f-949a5031457dR01